ACTING
Professiona

RAW FACTS
ABOUT ACTIN
AND THE ACTING IN

ROBERT C

University of Cal

ooo

NATIO

TO:

Pam	Charlie	Robin
Steve	Donna	Marcy
Bruce	Marc	Jeri
Bill	Dena	Jerry
Denise	Judy	Doug
Jeff	Astrid	Betty
Donna	Elaine	Penny
Eve	Michelle	Mark
Susie	Don	Sidney
Cathy	Jack	Tom
Jim	Richard	Margaret
Larry	Jon	Toni
Mike	Katie	Bill
Wayne	Bob	David
John	Linda	Oakley
	Ernie	

and above all, Annie—
May you all be the one in a hundred . . .

CONTENTS

∘ FOUR ∘

FOREWORD

Robert Cohen has done the theatrical profession a great service in writing this long-needed book which you are about to read. It is not only an extremely practical guide for aspiring actors and actresses, but a blessing undisguised for show business professionals. Ever since the first star was born, impresarios, actors, producers, directors, casting directors, agents, press agents, and drama coaches have been bombarded by career questions fired at them by young actors. Now at last those beleaguered elders can smile reassuringly and answer almost any such question with an authoritative and explicit, "Read *Acting Professionally* by Robert Cohen."

Having spent nearly my entire life in this fascinating and frustrating profession—performing in vaudeville, on Broadway, in radio, television and motion pictures, and then for many years as a film director, I can only wish this book had been available when I was a fledgling actor. However, thank the Muses, here it is now: a comprehensive guide for the bedeviled by a man who has obviously been through the fire.

To those of you who read *Acting Professionally* and feel only a sense of panic, be grateful. Mr. Cohen has probably saved you from a life of chasing rainbows—an extremely unfulfilling occupation.

To those of you who still choose to dedicate yourselves to an acting career, good luck. You may never see your name in lights but neither does a stonemason who beams with pride at the smoke curling from the fireplace he has built nor a chef who peeks from his kitchen and smiles contentedly at the diners savoring his creations—to wit, the wise men who work at what they love not only for glory but also soul satisfaction.

So read on, ladies and gentlemen. If act you must, learn to act professionally—forewarned and forearmed, unlike actors past, who had not this map to guide them.

Richard Quine

RICHARD QUINE *is eminently qualified to comment on "acting professionally": child star in vaudeville, leading man on the Broadway stage and on radio, Hollywood actor, TV producer, and director of films such as* My Sister Eileen, The World of Suzie Wong, Synanon, Hotel, *and* Bell, Book and Candle.

ONE

INTRODUCTION

This book seeks to give practical information and advice to people who are considering acting professionally as a lifetime career. It is odd to think that thousands of aspiring actors graduate from drama schools and institutes every year, well-versed in Shakespeare and Stanislavski and yet totally ignorant of the realities of the theatrical marketplace. It is not an exaggeration to say that no other profession is so totally misunderstood by the young people who are anxious to enter it.

The reason for this misunderstanding is clear, however. To many adolescents, acting is the most glamorous of all careers. Posh Beverly Hills parties, fan clubs, Fifth Avenue penthouses, fame, and notoriety: the hope of these entices thousands of youngsters every year to put aside such commonplace goals as motherhood, carpentry, and bookkeeping, and to get on the stage or screen in any way they can. Thousands more delve into theatre or film as art, and study diligently to become the Bernhardts, Chaplins, or Oliviers of their generation. Almost to a man these young people, blinded by ignorance and idealistic fantasies, blunder into a bitterly competitive marketplace where they are crushed like birds in a hurricane. It is a pathetic experience, and the fact that it is well enough known to have become a cliche of American soap operas does not prevent thousands every year from entering into it. This book seeks to replace fantasies with realities and to assist young actors in making their experiences, if not always successful, at least of some practical value.

The book examines the contemporary professional situations from both within and without, and combines wide-ranging research with the insights gained from comprehensive personal experiences. The author* has realistically studied all major acting media in New York and Los Angeles and in writing has been guided entirely by the goal of accuracy in a field filled with gossip, misinformation, and the fantasies of people too starstruck, or too "artstruck," to believe the evidence they see daily.

The professional theatre is an industry. Hollywood is an industry. There are procedures and protocols that are as strict in these industries as in the washing machine industry. The familiar image used to describe the entertainment industries is "the jungle." Yes, you will find vice, lechery, corruption, avarice, deception, and hypocrisy there, just as you are likely to find them anywhere in America's corporate structure; and you may well find them more vicious, bitter, and violent than elsewhere simply because the passions aroused are fiercer and the lust for success is greater. If you are unaware of "the jungle" you may find yourself gobbled alive almost before you start; if you are aware, you will at least know what to avoid and where the action really is.

In this book I* am trying to describe the profession of acting in specific and objective detail. I am not, myself, an actor, nor have I ever tried to become one; I have no personal axe to grind, no bitterness to mask, and no particular elation to convey. Yet for the past fifteen years I have been living, writing, and working side by side with young persons actively involved in the professional theatre and film industries. I do have a certain bias, which is shared by virtually everyone in the industries, and that is to describe the acting profession without promoting it. If I can discourage 90 percent of my readers from attempting a theatrical or film career, I will have done some service, for more than that number will surely fail in any case, and I will have spared them the trauma. On the other hand, for those talented and hardy souls who are willing and

*Hereafter the author uses the editorial "we," not out of affectation but to acknowledge his indebtedness to the hundreds of actors, agents, directors, casting directors, and producers who have contributed their knowledge and experience to this work.

able to commit themselves to an acting career, I think you will find the suggestions and information in this book helpful. Suggestions, of course, are not rules. There are no rules to success in the theatre, and no proven path to stardom; if there were this book would not really be necessary. There are only decisions to be made, and this book is intended to help you make the best ones.

The economics
of the acting profession

Young people have, as a matter of course, either of two economic goals in mind when they begin to think of acting professionally.

The first goal is "adolescent." They wish to be movie stars and make piles of money.

The second is "mature." They scorn piles of money in favor of artistic respectability. They disdain Hollywood and maybe New York, and opt for a steady job with a modest repertory company and a reasonable salary. "Doing one's thing," particularly one's acting thing, they say, is enough reward.

And so it would be — if they could do it. The truth, of course, is that *both* of these visions are remote fantasies, since the supply of actors so exceeds the demand for them that an actor really must be one in a hundred to get *any* job. One in a hundred, *literally.*

The idea that there are hundreds of paid acting positions in America's regional theatres and that these are, as a matter of routine, available to professionally inexperienced young actors is a popular undergraduate rumor with no foundation whatever. A little research shows that it is easier to land a job in a TV series than as a regular performer for a Louisville repertory company. A young actor with superb college drama credentials should no more expect to get a paid acting job than a political science graduate should expect to become a United States senator.

The fact is that there are frighteningly few jobs of any kind available in the American theatre. To presume that you might be hired because you do not ask for very much money is frankly unrealistic. In the first place almost everybody in the theatre is just as hungry for work as you are; and in the second, the unions will keep you from working at less than a minimum wage. Since *thousands* are willing to work *at* minimum, your economic bargaining power as a beginner is nonexistent. Your generosity in offering to work for a pittance will go unrewarded and unacknowledged, and you will learn another thing: there is not that much money in acting anyway!

How much do actors really make? There are over 24,000 members in the Screen Actors' Guild (which handles all film and filmed television acting) and half of them reside in the Hollywood area. Of the Hollywood SAG members, only 4000 earned as much as $3500 in 1969. From that gross figure must be deducted taxes, agents' commissions, and the expenses of commuting to interviews and working sessions. In other words, *in 1969 only one out of three working, professional, unionized Hollywood actors made as much as $200 a month,* an income on which it is hard to live. Two out of three made less, or nothing.

The average income figure for professional stage actors in New York is even more dismal, with the median income down below $2000 per year and unemployment averaging between 75 and 85 percent at most times. Unemployment is frequently *above* 85 percent. The salaries of working performers are often ridiculously low. Until the Equity strike of 1970, actors working off-Broadway were paid on a scale that, for most shows, began at $80 weekly. In New York, $80 a week is barely a subsistence wage; hardly enough to feed yourself and a poodle on. Yet the "textbook" of off-Broadway productions explains to the potential producer: "Almost always the cast is hired for the equity minimum, and their greater remuneration comes from the opportunity to work . . . "* Still, $80 is something, you say; and there *are* hundreds of young actors struggling to live on it. But then of course the $80 ($50 when you've deducted taxes and expenses) is not steady. After ten weeks the show closes and the paycheck disappears. How much have you saved up?

There is more money in Hollywood than New York, in general, and the figures there, when you first see them, seem gigantic. The scale pay for filmed television performing is $138 a day, for example, and a week's minimum paycheck is $483. Eyes glisten, for who couldn't make a living getting $138 a day every now and then?

*Donald Farber, *From Option to Opening* (New York: DBS Publications, 1968), p. 99.

The problem is the "every now and then." It involves an implicit multiplication which says, "All I have to do is only work five or ten days a month and . . .," but we are already in the area of fantasy, because *nobody* starts out by working regularly five or ten days a month. You may start out with three days in January, two more in March, a day in November, and another two in December, and you still will not clear $1000 until the residual checks finally come in. At that, you could quadruple those figures, including residuals, and you would still make more on welfare. This is what is happening to the two out of three in Hollywood who cannot make that $138 a day add up to more than $3,500 a year.

It is said that the theatre and film industries are currently in a state of economic depression. You should be aware, however, that this has been said steadily for the past half-century. It looks as if this country, the only developed nation in the Western world which does not provide regular governmental subsidies for the performing arts, will continue to be cursed with the boom-or-bust economics of Broadway and Hollywood for a long time. In both cities, by the way, the technical positions are as highly unionized as the acting positions and just as depressed financially. In the fall of 1970 the International Alliance of Theatrical Stage Employees reported 38 percent unemployment in the Hollywood-Los Angeles area, with some guilds reporting as high an unemployment figure as 50 percent. The International Alliance of (stage) Laborers, Local 727 (Hollywood), reported in 1971 that membership had dropped from 480 to 330 in the previous eighteen months because of the paucity of jobs. The union head explained: "A number of members are on relief, some are receiving welfare, some food stamps, some have exhausted their unemployment insurance."

In addition one must remember that for every union actor pounding the pavements in search of work, there is a non-union would-be badgering friends for jobs, information, help, a foot in the door. There are 330 U.S. college drama departments, graduating each year thousands of drama majors, many of whom have hopes for a career in professional acting. Another 600 schools have drama programs (but no major) and send another thousand or two graduates into the theatre every year. In addition there are professional schools and high schools sending forth more aspirants toward a career. These people are all your competition. They include many hundreds who are talented, hardworking, dedicated, and backed by glowing reviews from the Denver Post, the New Haven Register, and the Fresno Bee. They all have the same idea you do—to make it into show business—and they may even be more cut-throat about it than you are.

The art of the acting profession

It is clear that most actors live (if one calls it that) severely below the established poverty level. Further, lack of money creates enormous problems for people who not only have to live, eat, and stay healthy, but must dress well, look well, buy photographs, and drive around to auditions. Still, the financial deprivation is one that most actors are willing to put up with — at least for a while — because they are pursuing something far more important than economics. They are pursuing their "art." Sadly, however, the industry will almost certainly disappoint their "mature" artistic hopes as well as their "adolescent" yen for fame and riches.

A well-known film producer used to send his cast and crew a telegram on the first day of shooting for each picture. The message was "Forget art, make money." "Forget" was not the word he wanted, but it was one that Western Union would send over their lines. Most producers live by this message, and a huge amount of purely commercial claptrap is marketed both in Hollywood and New York, and even by the resident regional theatres.

A review of the film "The Love Machine" in *Variety* made this significant point: "The secret of a film like this, rarely spoken outside of inner sanctums, is that if it were better written, better directed, and better acted, it would probably fail." The industry's prime goal is to make money and your value to the industry is determined precisely by how much money you can make for it. Art is a secondary consideration in most industry enterprises, and no "new wave" or "new theatre" has made a lasting dent in this principle.

Certainly there are many people in both Hollywood and New York who make money and art at the same time, but there are also many who make money without making art, and who are only too happy to admit it. Here is the schizophrenia of show business. It is both commerce and creativity, and the two are almost invariably in conflict. With every act of genuine creation, there is a follow-up of massive, non-creative exploitation. Originality, which is the hallmark of the artist, is an invitation to financial disaster; and those who call the tune — angels, sponsors, and corporate producers — are all too eager to copy last year's success rather than experiment with an untried commodity. When the price of a big Broadway show runs close to a million dollars, and of a film up to twenty million, the producers will tend to imitate whatever previously successful models they can find. Thus are the new genres created: the "widower" TV series, the "folk Jewish" musicals and the sexploitation films. Successful plays, movies, and television shows replicate like cancer cells, and films, for example, that are advertised as "this year's *Easy Rider*" dominate an industry that often cannot tolerate truly artistic creation.

There is a common impression in the business that, for acting, New York is a more artistic milieu than Hollywood, and regional repertory more artistic than New York. Like all generalizations, however, this can be counted as only 51 percent correct. There are artists in Hollywood and on the other hand, there is vice, graft, exploitation, indolence, and greed throughout *every* phase of the theatre. In general, you are going to have to tread carefully between art and money, and you will have to hang on to your integrity with an iron grip.

If you have guessed that the foregoing information is meant to alarm you, you have guessed correctly. Later on, we will have some nice things to say about acting as a profession, but at this point nothing would be more misleading than to encourage young people in a profession that really has no room for them. There is a standard piece of advice given by producers to aspiring actors: "Don't bother." We agree with this advice completely, on the grounds that the people who are going to "make it" will disregard us anyway.

TWO

WHAT WILL YOU NEED?

If you are going to make it—that is, if you are going to make a livelihood as an actor—then you must possess the following:

Talent

A charming/fascinating/interesting/likable hateful/definable personality

Certain physical characteristics

Proper training

Experience

Contacts

Commitment and will to succeed

A healthy attitude and capacity for psychological adjustment

Freedom from entanglements and inhibitions

Good information, advice, and help

Luck

Quite likely you rebel at seeing some of these items listed, such as "contacts," "certain physical characteristics," or "freedom from inhibitions." We do not mean these items in the usual melodramatic sense. You do not have to be the son of a cameraman, or a Miss Georgia contestant, and you certainly do not have to sleep with the casting director, to succeed in an acting career. But we stand firm on the importance of developing contacts, becoming flexible in your acting, and caring for your body. Without these interests you probably do not have the attitude requisite to becoming a performer. Considered singly, these are the basic ingredients for professional work.

Talent

We are happy to report that, after fifteen years of study, we still find that the first requirement for success is talent. It is of incomparably greater importance than any other factor. Talent is the *sine qua non* of a performer. Certainly there are those who make a brief appearance on the professional scene without it, but lasting success comes only to those who have it. Do *you* have it? That is the question on which neuroses are based. Here are some basic guidelines for answering that question.

As a performer, you must be outstanding *now*. In college or neighborhood plays, you should be getting major roles or being considered for them. If after two or three years of training as an actor you still are unsuccessful at getting these roles in college or community theatre productions, you should reconsider. "Major" roles, of course, are not defined just by size, but as the roles you *want* to play—the roles you think you *ought* to play. While it may be perfectly true that "there are no small roles, only small actors," the fact remains that in a non-professional situation only a major role will fully expand and test your abilities. The size of a role is not of primary consequence; the depth, breadth, wit, passion, individuality, and "electricity" of the role: these are the characteristics which determine whether it is "major." A policeman who comes in at the end to arrest somebody, or Morton in *Henry IV* Part II, who describes at the beginning of the play everything that has happened since the end of Part I: these are certainly roles that can be played magnificently or badly, but in themselves they are hardly an accurate test of future potential.

The people whom we have seen rise to successful careers and even stardom in the past fifteen years were without significant exception recognized as *extraordinarily* talented at the very beginning. While craft and experience can be acquired along the way, talent, where it exists, shows up almost immediately.

On the other hand, that extraordinary talent does not at all mean perfection of performance or anything even close to it. Extraordinary talented people have been sunk in one disaster after another. They perform badly, they cannot be heard, they are not believable, they do the same thing over and over, they become too fat or too thin, they are always committing some terrible error or other, and they often reap the scorn of their peers and sometimes even their directors. But they always get cast. Hardly anyone had a good thing to say about Stacy Keach, Jr., when he was a student at Yale Drama School, for example. The other acting students gravely discussed his near-fatal problems and his teachers despaired of his ability to grow under their tutelage. But he was cast in every leading male role available the year he was there, and he is now a stage and film star. His talent was so enormous that no director could turn him down when it came time to cast his play, and so obvious that it could only incite jealousy among his peers.

Extraordinary talent manifests itself in many ways. It is always accompanied by a great inner confidence: in fact, some say that it is *only* that. Confidence is the power a person has over his own personality; it allows him to accept criticism and at the same time to rise above it. It allows him to believe in the reality of his own performance even when and if no one else does. An actor may have all kinds of doubts about his potential for career success, but he may not doubt that "he is an actor," that he can act. He must believe it in his bones. He must believe it in every interview and every audition, and believe it so much that his belief shows even though he makes no *effort* to show it. It is the power which makes him galvanize everything that he is as a person, and everything he has learned as an actor, into an exciting and apparently artless performance or audition.

"Talent is not definable, but it is recognizable." This is a common statement and it makes sense. Talent is variously described as magnetism, electricity, stage presence. We think it is those qualities that make a person *project without pushing.* Such "presence" carries through offstage as well as onstage: it involves the way you dress, talk, communicate, live, eat, and look. Onstage it involves your ability to communicate naturally with the simplest and most basic tools: speech, gesture, and body action. Because acting is basically an art that draws on the subconsious, an actor's *offstage* behavior often reveals "presence" as well. This is why we say that talent is frequently recognizable in daily life.

If an actor has magnetism, he stands out in any performance, no matter how much of an amateur he may be. He is watched. He may make mistakes, but he is watched. And he is judged. He is great or terrible, he wears too much make-up, he is too effeminate, he is sensational, he is loud, he is incomprehensible, he is this or he is that—but he is never boring. Chances are we would like to meet him after the show, because he seems to be a fascinating person. He is talented.

If you have been in or around the theatre for a few years and nobody ever thought about you in this way, and if *you* have not thought about yourself in this way, then—we won't say this again—it is time to think of bricklaying or veterinary medicine.

Talent means all this and more still. It *can* mean, in addition:

—That a person sings, dances, juggles, tells jokes, or does striptease, backflips, handsprings, or T'ai ch'ai. Most talented people can do some of these; many more think they are talented because they can do one or two. A person who is genuinely talented need not be able to sing on key but can probably "sell" a song if called upon to do so. The more talents a person has in his portfolio, obviously, the more employable he is.

—That a person can communicate nuances clearly yet subtly. That he can vary inflection and timing so as to communicate what his director wants, without excessive coaching or reworking. Whether he does this by technique or instinct is not the concern of this book, but that he must be able to do it, everyone agrees. And he must be able to do it rapidly, particularly during an audition.

—That a person has a flexible, mobile, and expressive voice and body. These are the actor's tools. At the outset, the actor must be in possession of an expressive speaking voice: one that communicates what is between the lines, that connotes something beyond the mere words spoken. Similarly the body: the talented person communicates in movement and repose more than a mannequin. Sex appeal is obviously related to this, and although that is not by a long shot the whole story, it is clear that an audience sensually intrigued is an audience already on its way to admiring and relishing a performance. Casting directors have never been oblivious to this. You should not be, either.

—That a person stands out in a crowd, or a chorus, without seeming to try. Because of his energy, or his deep-set eyes, or the way he tosses his head, curls his lip, or studiously reflects, his presence alone draws attention. It is hard to imagine cultivating this quality in oneself. At the same time, it is such a quality which distinguishes certain people even when lined up at a ticket counter. Can one imagine not looking twice at Richard Burton, or Jacqueline Bisset, or Elliot Gould? It is not a matter of beauty necessarily, but of personal excitement.

—That a person is relaxed in front of others, or when performing for others, and enjoys such performing. This enjoyment is said to result from an exhibitionistic instinct and nothing in our experience contradicts that. Though an actor may be as shy as anyone else—and not a few of them are painfully shy—some part of his personality relishes contact with others, even via the formal medium of theatre or film. The desire for fame need not be great, nor need there be a mammoth desire for great public or financial success. But there must be some strong, basic impulse toward reaching one's natural audience, small or large, and stimulating them.

These are all aspects of "talent," and the word is often used to denote one or more of them. There are no firm prerequisites for "making it" in show business, but the necessity for talent comes as close as any possibly could.

Personality

We list this second and there are shrieks. "What does my personality have to do with it? I'm an actor, not a prostitute! Use me for my talent—for what I can do; not for what I am! My personality is my own business!" Yes, it is, and your business is acting.

American film and theatre performances are dominated by the Stanislavski/Strasberg/*cinema verité* school of acting. Whether one is happy or sad about this, it remains true: so totally true that even directors and producers who publicly condemn "the method" nevertheless refuse to cast any actor who does not follow its basic precepts. They are, of course, unaware of this, but it is nonetheless true. Particularly in film and television work, the actor is cast largely on the basis of his "personal quality." The major casting decisions are made without, or before, auditions. For one role fifty actresses may be interviewed. The three or four that have the right personality for the role are then given copies of the text to read a-loud for the producer. Thus, 92 percent of the decision is based on the candidate's personal behavior, and 8 percent on her talent and ability beyond that. Professional stage work is determined more by auditioning than interviewing, but the importance of a stageworthy personality—one suited to the role, of course—is still enormously great.

The reasons for this are many. Primarily, directors are seeking naturalness and they are commercially pressured to get it quickly. Unlike Stanislavski himself, the modern American stage director must get good characterizations in a matter of three or four weeks; the television director has at most a couple of days and frequently only about fifteen minutes. On a normal television shooting schedule, the actor will appear on the set, with his lines learned and ready to shoot, at eight o'clock in the morning. He has had no instructions whatever, has had the script for maybe twenty-four hours, and meets the director minutes before the actual shooting. There is a quick rehearsal, the blocking is set, and the director may give a reading or direction or two. Minutes later the scene is filmed and they are on to the next. Clearly there is no time to work at developing a character. Television directors, therefore, *must* use your personality as a basis for casting. The foundation of this short-order work is simply Stanislavski's "Magic If." What would you do "if" you were Linda in *Room 222* and the principal were yelling at you and your boyfriend were trying to get your attention? Linda will do it as *you* would do it, and Linda comes out looking a lot like you, which is why they cast you in the first place; that is how they saw Linda.

Acting in films and on the stage gives the actors and director more time to work out characterizations; still the premium, in this country, is on naturalism in portrayal. Casting directors tend to look for personal characteristics and idiosyncrasies which can be carried into the role. The film camera, which penetrates ruthlessly through all your high school and college "schtick" acting, comes up with the real you. If that is not what they want, you do not get the job. Even our stage acting is based on realism for the most part, particularly when compared to the European theatre. The development of *cinema verité* in films and improvisational acting on stage has made this even more apparent as the 60's turn into the 70's. And while no one could argue successfully that realism demands absolute fidelity to one's own personality, it certainly is true that what you have to start with in that regard is a major factor in the performance you will give.

What is a good acting personality? It is no one thing in particular, but it is something definable in general terms. You are shy, you are fascinating, you are profound, you are aggressive, you are hostile, you are nasty, you are fiery, you are sensual, you are youthful, you are idealistic, you are wacky, you are serene. Plain ordinary old NICE will get you nowhere. Thousands of aspiring actors have "blown" an interview simply by being polite and forgotten. Yes, there is an "interview technique." A hundred actors will explain, "I didn't get the job because I don't play their games at the interview. I'm just not that kind of person." But it's not a game. Interview technique is simply letting them see just *what* kind of person you *are*. If that is hidden behind a lot of "pleased-to-meet-yous" and "thank-you-very-muches" you will find that you have not only lost your chance at a further audition, but that you have in fact been playing *your own* game—the parents' and teachers' and business school interview game —and that for perhaps the first time in your life it was the wrong game to play. The casting game is the business of projecting (for you) and discovering (for them) your real self, whatever that may be.

Successful actors are not bland people. That is not to say that they are brash, either. Most of our acquaintance are people of depth, sensitivity, dedication, and artistry. Their personalities are not applied for the sake of calling attention to themselves. The surest way to lose your personality is to fake one. Your real personality will follow you in every role you play; it will become your trademark. In the classic days of Hollywood such trademarks were Bogart's toughness, John Wayne's reckless virility, Fonda's sensitive passion, Marilyn Monroe's soft, defenseless sexuality, Marlon Brando's vulnerable egotism, W. C. Fields's cynicism, Mae West's leering defiance, Grace Kelly's poise, and Clark Gable's cockiness. These were not "put on" personalities, they were intrinsic to their owners and vital to their success. The personalities of today's rising stars are more subtle, perhaps, but just as ingrained in their performances, even in varied characterizations. One need only remember Dustin Hoffman's defensive smirk in *The Graduate* and *Midnight Cowboy* or Sandy Dennis's pouting in *Virginia Woolf* and *The Out-of-Towners*. The day of the "personality actor" is far from over; and in fact there is no indication that it is even beginning to end.

You cannot create your personality—your stage personality—but you can liberate it. What are your personal characteristics? What do others see in you? Find out and let these characteristics come out. Do not worry about "your good features versus your bad features." Just have features. Don't be afraid to be different. Don't opt for the ordinary, for the nice. Don't try to be what you think they want you to be. Don't worry about yourself. Be proud of yourself. Like yourself. If you do not, it is hard to see how somebody else will.

There is one final aspect regarding your personality in which casting directors and producers are interested. Do they like you and want to know you better? The best way to know you better is to hire you and work with you. Too often young aspirants ignore the obvious. Directors and producers are people too; they are interested in art and money, of course, but they want to enjoy their work, just as you do. If they like you they are more inclined to want to hire you. They certainly will not hire you on that basis alone, but it helps. There is no sure way to be liked, but if you can combine vicacity with sensitivity, and charm with sincerity, you shouldn't have much trouble.

Physical characteristics

No cry in the theatre is raised as strongly as that against "type casting." The art of acting, it is often maintained, is the actor's ability to essay a wide range of roles of varying ages, historical periods, dramatic characteristics, and styles. Repertory, it is said, encourages actors to alternate between Molière comedy, Tennessee Williams romanticism, and Shakespearean tragedy—from the youthful Romeo to the aged Northumberland. No doubt. But most casting in the professional theatre and in film and TV today is done by physical type. Until that changes the following advice should be of value.

Your physical characteristics are partly controllable, partly intrinsic. Your height, age, race, and bone structure are largely unchangeable. Your weight, dress, hair style and appearance give you certain latitudes for control. What should you aim for?

As with personality, there is no classic norm. The ideal of perfect beauty, nowadays, is as worthless as the "nice" personality, and the waiting rooms of New York and Hollywood casting offices are filled with hundreds of hopeless beauties from the charm schools, beauty contests, and super-elegant men's shops of America. As with personality, the premium is on a specific, memorable and definable "look" and that look should be within a specific time-honored "type."

Types exist, and they exist today exactly as they were a hundred years ago. Male and female "children," "young leading men," "ingenues," "leading men," "leading women," "character men and comedians," and "character women and comediennes." There are subgroups, but these eight remain the basic ones. The *Players' Directory* which is a publication of photographs of all working actors in the Los Angeles area, and an invaluable tool in the casting process, divides actors into these categories for the convenience of producers. If you aren't in the right category, you won't even be looked at.

"Children" designates actors twelve years old and younger. "Preteens" are those from thirteen to fifteen, and "teens" from sixteen to nineteen. Ordinarily these character types are not involved in romantic affairs. On stage, anyway.

"Ingenues" (girls) and "young leading men" are in the "first love" category. Usually they are in their early to mid-twenties and send off vibrations of youth, innocence, and charm.

"Leading men" and "leading ladies" are, by contrast, wiser, more experienced lovers; glamorous, romantic, mature, sophisticated, in their mid-twenties to mid-forties and beyond.

"Character men," "character women," "comedians," and "comediennes" are not romantic in a conventional sense. They are usually older, and their appearance is likely to be distinctive rather than attractive.

Notice that types are not defined solely by age, but also by a position on some sort of sexual scale. This is simply an accurate reading of the typing that is done in theatre and film casting. No one assumes that an unattractive character cannot be portrayed in a romantic role (as in *Marty*). It is just that to do so is to cast deliberately against type, and such casting is rarely done except when a specific play or film calls for it. Since the time of Aristophanes, audiences have expected ingenues to be young and innocent, lovers to be beautiful and sensitive, and comics to be old and usually pudgy. Few casting directors wish to disappoint an audience.

It is important to find your type, if only to get yourself in the right chapter of the *Players' Guide*. More than that, you are categorized in the producer's mind; you are provided with a convenient label—a basis for comparison with other actors. You protest: you are an individual, not a type! If you are Laurence Olivier, you do not need a label. If you are not, you must start somewhere. Even "male" or "female" is a label, and you can be at least a little more specific than that.

You must decide whether you can play juveniles, for example. Either you can play fourteen-year-olds or you cannot. Perhaps you can do a passable job, of course, but can you do better than a *real* fourteen-year-old? If so, sign up, because producers hate to use real fourteen-year-olds if they can avoid it. (They really hate to use anybody younger than eighteen, because they must pay to have a tutor on the set. If you are nineteen and can play twelve, they will love you.)

You should clearly be a character actor or not. If you are ten pounds overweight, you are dead. Either lose it, or gain twenty more. If you look like an IBM executive or a nineteen-year-old hippie you are fine, but if you look half like one and half like the other you are in trouble. If you are ugly, don't worry about hiding it. Cultivate it. Use what you have to create a distinctive appearance. Be happy with what you are. Make it count. One of the most successful young actors today has a prominent hare-lip scar and is half bald at twenty-nine. Neither is masked by surgery or Hair-Anew. There is no "bad" appearance except a bland, characterless, typeless one.

For leading men and women, the old ideals are out the window. It is no longer necessary for men to be tall, dark, and handsome, or for women to be platinum blondes with hourglass figures. You might cultivate an "in" look. Currently that happens to be wiry-Jewish for men (Elliot Gould, Dustin Hoffman) and tomboyish lanky for women (Carrie Snodgrass, Ali MacGraw). Any month, however, it is liable to change. The actual style is unimportant so long as the appearance works. If you are a leading man, you must appeal to women; women, vice versa. There are all kinds of ways of doing that, and for some it comes more naturally than others. But you *can* do it if you're willing to devote some time, a little money, and a frankly self-critical attitude to the problem. The main difference between professional and amateur theatre auditions, it seems to us, is the total lack of concern amateurs have over their personal appearance. They are simply blind to the realities, and often appear to be waiting for some Star of Bethlehem to shine over them and so point them out to the director. The folly of this approach need not be further discussed.

Cultivate distinction in appearance. Separate yourself from the rest of your friends. Find an exciting hairstyle for yourself, a natural one if that is the current trend, but one that looks better on you than anybody else, and one that is not seen too much. Dress distinctively. If you are a girl and you like going around in jeans and body shirts, then get some that fit right, and some great belts and boots, and look terrific. Extravagance and propriety are not worth a plug nickel in this business, but distinction *in your own terms* is. Find yourself, and find in yourself a unique appearance that will intrigue others.

One necessary word about your weight, however. If you should lose weight, do so. Most Americans are overweight. Most performers are not. There is a rather direct correlation between chubby actors and those who do not get work. Particularly in film and television, where the camera adds ten or fifteen pounds to you anyway, the premium is and has always been on slim, lissome people. Take a look on television programs at the young people playing the three-line parts. Are they fat? No. These are the parts you will be going for if you're just starting out. This becomes even more true if you are offering yourself as a dancer or singer. Sophie Tucker and Kate Smith are rarities, and not for general emulation. Unless you are completely sure you want to make it as a fat character actor, take off those extra twenty pounds, cinch in your waist, and do not worry if your parents wonder why you are so skinny. The Bieler diet and the so-called "water diet" are favorites among actors for quick and lasting weight loss.

How do you *use* your appearance? It precedes you in every interview and every audition. Your photographs are your letters of introduction. No actor can begin to look for work without a set of photographs, and so we have a separate section on the subject. Read it thoroughly in conjunction with this one. Your photographs should show just what your appearance should show: originality, vitality, distinctiveness. If you look like something out of a high school yearbook, the chances are that you will never be heard of again.

Training and experience

You need it. No matter how naturally talented, attractive, sexy, and individual you are, you will flop in the audition if you do not know what to do. In the old days, a decade or more ago, actors without formal training were the rule. Now they are very definitely the exception. Training in the art and craft of acting is a virtual necessity for a successful career, and if you *are* hired at first without it, you will need it thereafter. There are six major sorts of training you may take: high school drama classes, college drama or film classes, commercial acting classes, studio classes, apprenticeships, or private instruction. Each of these groups is populated with enough master teachers and inspiring creative artists to train a cast of thousands.

Good teachers pop up in the craziest places, and there is no reason why a high school drama class cannot be a stimulating and effective training program. Some undoubtedly are. Frequently high schools are fortunate in hiring out-of-work (or given-up-in-disgust) professional actors who transmit their knowledge masterfully to eager young people. That is a good start. And there are many fine drama programs in colleges across the country which provide basic training in acting as well as other theatre skills and subjects. Yale University, Carnegie Tech University, Catholic University, New York University, USC and UCLA have developed, over the years, fine reputations within the professional theatre. The author of this volume is currently on another campus which seeks to offer professional instruction in acting and directing. Many more universities in the American heartland have also built reputations over the years: Michigan, Wayne State, Indiana, Oklahoma, Texas, Colorado, Washington, Cornell, and Syracuse, to name but a few. And while college graduates ten years ago may have sought to hide their diplomas from theatrical employers, they now may proudly sport not only BA's but MA's, MFA's and even PhD's without embarrassment. For as we shall see, the professional theatre and film world has moved into an informal alliance with the universities, and while the old resentments occasionally persist, two worlds have moved into a closer proximity.

Why is this? For one reason, most Americans go to college now, and those college students who plan to be actors now study drama instead of chemistry or political science. Drama, which has been introduced as a subject of legitimate study only in the last forty years, is now a "major" on literally hundreds of campuses, and graduate degrees in Theatre, Theatre Arts, Filmmaking, Drama and Dramatic Art are now commonplace.

Secondly, the "educational theatre" establishment has itself become much more professionalized, and experienced professional actors and directors are being sought eagerly to provide on-campus instruction. Many university drama departments, in fact, suffer a split between the professionally oriented faculty, and the older, academically oriented one. It is imperative that prospective students determine the climate in the drama department of their choice before signing on: they may find that students and professors interested in professional theatre or film work are discriminated against in favor of prospective speech teachers and Racine scholars.

Thirdly, the professional theatre has to some extent become more "educationalized." Films in this country are now a relevant reflection of culture and ideology. Successful films are more and more directed toward philosophical and social ends. Television has experimented with "relevance," and even if that experiment has disappointed most critics, the general level of all media entertainment has become more thoughtful than in past decades. A simple comparison of *Room 222* (c.1970) to *Our Miss Brooks* (c.1960) *or Mister Peepers* (c.1950) proves the point. So-called educational television, public broadcasting, and subsidized regional theatre experimentation call for intelligent, broadly trained actors as well as a college-level audience.

So college experience, and college experience in drama or drama-related discipline, while not essential, has become at least a desirable part of an actor's training. A degree is sometimes helpful, and a graduate degree sometimes more helpful, although it is hard to ascertain this by actual records. But it is also true that no one has ever been denied a role because he lacked a college degree.

Should you go to college? If you are in college, should you stay? Should you go on to graduate school? These are vital questions for many students.

In general, if you are planning a career as a professional actor, you might follow these precepts:

If you have graduated from high school, desire to go to college, and have been accepted at a college with a good drama department, go. Major in drama and act in every play you can. If the college has a film department, get involved there also.

Stay in college as long as you feel you are really growing as an actor. Measure this on a year-to-year, not day-to-day, basis.

If at any time in your college career six or eight months pass during which you feel you have gotten everything out of the college that you can, that you have surpassed most of the other students in your talent and craft, and that the directors and instructors do not have much left to teach you and are not inspiring you, think about leaving.

If you feel ready to take the professional plunge, do so. You will never be more ready.

If, however, you still wish to get your degree, see if you can transfer to a big metropolitan campus such as NYU, UCLA, USC, or CUNY and finish your degree work while trying to get involved on the side professionally. This is hazardous and full of problems, but it beats wasting another year or two around the old quad redoing your old characterizations. At least you will be thrown into another crowd and forced up against fresh competition and criticism.

If, having received your BA in drama, you still feel the need of further academic training and a higher degree, go to graduate school. But beware. Graduate schools are full of persons without the guts to really try for a career. By now you should know whether you want to go for a professional career or a teaching career. Indecision at this point could blow your chances for either. However, if you wish to continue working towards the profession while getting an MFA at the same time, we offer two suggestions:

Go to the very best graduate school you can. Ask your teachers what they are: they vary from year to year.

Go to a graduate school within commuting distance of New York or Los Angeles. No matter how fine a school may be in Kansas or Alaska, you will leave there with your PhD in hand at twenty-six and miles behind a sixteen-year-old graduate of Hollywood High or New York's High School of Performing Arts.

Do not ever forget that you are trying to enter the most competitive profession that exists, and that only the very best academic credentials mean anything whatever.

The foregoing only applies to students planning professional careers. In another chapter we discuss adequate preparation for teaching careers, which is naturally quite different.

What does a college education do for you? As far as your dramatic instruction, it is probably going to be pretty good. Some colleges have fine acting instructors with whom you may study regularly for your entire four-year academic career. Others allow you to study acting only for a year or two, but then give you credit for workshop plays and major productions. Many give you professional direction, and others let you work with regional companies and actually play roles in professional productions. Virtually all the major colleges have facilities for theatrical production which make professional producers livid with anger; 80-dimmer 10-preset electronic lighting boards which far surpass Broadway standards are common on US campus stages. Generally the equipment in the colleges is advanced beyond anything you may work with for the rest of your life —even if you make it.

Does a college degree help you get a job? Yes and no. Or rather, no and yes, because the negative somewhat outweighs the positive. No New York or Hollywood producer will ask you for evidence of a college degree or even a college education, and few actors even bother to list their degrees on their professional résumés. But producers and directors do want to know you can act, and college acting experience, if they like you to begin with, is helpful, if not impressive. In fact, a college degree may be your ultimate tool in breaking into the union. Present Screen Actors' Guild regulations require the producer to pay a $100 fine for casting a non-union actor in a film role, unless that actor can prove that he is "equivalently trained." A college degree in drama, together with a letter of recommendation from a drama professor, is accepted evidence that the student is a genuinely dedicated actress, for example, and not a super-friendly barmaid from last night's post-production bash.

Finally, it is through college drama departments that young actors may get their first job, via the intermediate step of Theatre Communications Group (TCG) auditions. The TCG auditions, supplemented now by the University Resident Theatre Association auditions, which are described further on, are held each year to bring together the best university drama students with directors of regional theatres. They are an important step for many actors, and accessible for the most part only to graduates of college drama programs.

On the other hand, a disadvantage of college theatres is that the amateur level is rarely surpassed. Principal performers can be excellent, but depth in casting is almost always lacking. The commonest problem is finding student actors capable of playing mature and old character parts. Pushing young actors into these roles creates a standard which perforce accepts "phony" acting, and lowers the overall production level. Too much work under these conditions allows actors and directors to assume lower standards and routinely excuse sloppy, amateurish work—or worse, to admire it, since "under the circumstances" it is all that can be achieved. If this is carried through to acting styles as a whole, then the college experience can be a disastrous one. The problem for the professionally oriented student acting (or directing) in colleges is to refuse to be dragged down by the amateurism and lack of commitment, real talent, and perfectionism that will in many cases surround him.

However, beyond the basic dramatic instruction, college in general offers many hidden advantages which are important to the young actor. A college education is a genuinely humanizing, broadening experience. It can introduce the actor to literature, history, psychology, politics, philosophy, economics, sociology, and the other arts and sciences that will be invaluable to him in his work. As an artist, the actor should also be a thoughtful, aware person. The college experience cultivates that awareness. The best actors are knowledgeable, bright people. That is one reason why so many of them are becoming involved in political and social action. The days of the "dumb blonde" and the "stupid stud" are past; today's actors, while not necessarily intellectuals, know how to think. They often branch into writing, producing, directing, and even politics. No one should skip or leave college *merely* out of impatience for a career, nor should a young actor, while enrolled in college, limit himself to acting courses and being in school plays. It is not necessary to examine every course in the college catalogue for its immediate importance or relevance to acting. The important thing is to learn, and to learn as much as you can about everything. It can't hurt, and it will probably help.

College, however, is only one form of education. There are hundreds of young actors without the money, the interest, or even the intelligence to go to college and for them, *and* for college dropouts, there are several non-collegiate alternatives. Principally there are commercial acting schools and studios. A few are listed in the appendix to this book, but a full list is available in the Los Angeles and New York yellow pages. (It is almost totally useless to go to a commercial school anywhere else, no matter how good it is, except for your own entertainment.)

Commercial schools vary enormously according to the interest of the instructor in his students and also according to his ability. Some, with famous names, are so past their usefulness that their classes are painful;

others, both famous and unknown, can be inspiring. Get recommendations from anybody you know: a personal interview or personal reference is probably the best possible way of locating a good instructor. But all commercial schools can be as good as the amount of work you are willing to do. You pay your money, you do your assignments, and you listen to the instructor. Just working with other professionally-minded students is extremely helpful. *All* aspiring actors, no matter what their prior training, should, if they can afford it, enroll in a good regular commercial acting class as soon as they hit New York or Los Angeles. For many, it's the first step into developing talent and contacts; for all, it is a way of continuing to grow in that long period before the first job or two.

In private instruction, one teacher works with students either singly or in small groups. Union office bulletin boards, trade journals, and occasionally the yellow pages list these along with larger acting schools. Many professional actors retain the regular services of an acting coach long after they become rich and famous; many have specialized coaches for acting, singing, voice, or speech, etc. Hiring a coach or signing on for private instruction is more expensive than taking an advertised class, and less valuable in terms of introducing you to large numbers of people. But if you can get with a coach who has a well-known clientele (and who is called upon, from time to time, by casting directors) you may have found yourself a very good deal.

You must, of course, use extreme care in choosing a commercial school or private teacher. Some offer the finest acting instruction available anywhere. The Neighborhood Playhouse School of the Theatre, the HB studio (run by the splendid team of Herbert Berghof and Uta Hagen), the Gene Frankel workshop: these and many others have sent hundreds of well-trained, superior actors into the profession. Others, unfortunately, are clip joints, pure and simple. The larger commercial schools have some placement services, but beware of any school or class that implies a job guarantee upon graduation. The courts are always after these people who advertise "Big pay, glamour awaits you!" and then soft-sell you for $465 (half the regular price, because you are so talented) for what amounts to a twenty-hour acting course taught by someone who once knew a Mousketeer. These schools, until they are shut down by the authorities, prey on the ignorance and fantasies of young actors and their families. It is easy to check the reliability of any school or acting coach, and local unions, agents, actors, and even the Better Business Bureau can provide information. Disbelieve all "too good to be true" promises: they are just that.

Apprenticeship with a repertory or summer stock company is a supremely good way of gaining theatre training, and this may supplement other forms of education. Various programs combine collegiate experience with professional repertory experience: for example the McKnight Fellowships involve study at the University of Minnesota and performance with the Minnesota (Tyrone Guthrie) Theatre Company. Apprenticeships with repertory companies are not easy to get, but summer stock apprenticeships are fairly easy to come by, and if you are good enough, you may end up with an Equity card in the process. Summer theatres, which are virtually all on the East Coast, and primarily in New England, are companies of professional actors that perform regularly for local and resort crowd audiences. Apprentices usually pay room, board, and a small tuition, live with the company, perform various backstage duties, and are occasionally permitted to perform small roles. The theatrical training is extraordinarily good for those who dedicate themselves to getting the most out of it, and frequently apprentices become full company members in succeeding years. The union regulations allow a summer stock producer to cast an apprentice an unlimited number of times in his first season with the company, but in his second year with the company, he must be signed to an Equity contract for his fourth role. An apprentice cannot remain with the company for a third year without being signed to Equity. There is some misunderstanding of this principle; merely being with a summer stock company for three years does not make you Equity; in order to be made Equity a summer stock producer has to want you so badly for the fourth production of your second year that he is willing to hire you at Equity prices (instead of getting you for free, as he has for the previous year and a half). If he does not want you that much, he simply will not cast you. But do not let this bother you. The training in working for a professional company is more than enough compensation. It is more than training; it is invaluable experience.

There is one final word to say about pre-professional training and experience. It can be overdone. College, acting classes, and the local community theatre can be very comfortable places. A lovely security envelops you—you are known, liked, respected, and well reviewed by the locals and by your teachers. But check your goals. If you want to move on, you had better go when you are ready rather than hang around merely because it is safe. Recognize the point of stagnation when the competition gets soft. There are actors who become so devoted to a favorite drama school or drama teacher that they study for eight or ten years without going out for a single audition, on the grounds that they are "not ready." The "professional student" is really psychologically aberrant. Recognize this trait in yourself, if it exists, and fight it. When you are ready to take the plunge, take it. The proper time is something only you can decide upon.

Contacts

Here we are. Contacts are the nemesis of the young unknown actor. You can whine, gripe, yell, and complain about it, but contacts are important—vital—in getting jobs in the theatre. But do not just quit on account of this: *think*. What does the term "contacts" actually mean?

Contacts are the people whom you know and who know you. If you were casting a play in a hurry and knew someone who was "just right" for the role, wouldn't you call him up and offer him a chance to audition? Would you really search through the drama classes at State University to find out if there were somebody else as good or better? No. You would call Harry and say, "Harry, I've got a part that's just right for you." And Harry would come over and read it, and if you liked his reading you would cast him in the role. It is not that you owe Harry a favor, but you like him, you envision him doing the part, and you can settle the matter in a quick, friendly way. Well, maybe you are the one-in-a thousand who would not call Harry, but the other 999 are in New York and Hollywood casting offices right now. You can either moan about it or work to beat it: the choice is yours.

So there is nothing mysterious about "contacts," and it is fruitless to play the sour grapes routine and say "I can't get anywhere because I don't have any pull." Of course you do not, but neither does anybody else just starting out. It is not as though your competition all went to school with Jerry Lewis's kids or swam in Dinah Shore's pool. Everybody, or almost everybody, starts off just as unknown and unwanted as you. If you do not have contacts, you simply have to develop them. It is as simple as that.

But wait a minute, you say. You don't believe in "It's not *what* you know but *who* you know." You want to make it "on your own." What does that mean? That you will be discovered? Where? At acting class? Singing in the shower? NOBODY ever made it "on his own." It always takes somebody else, and that somebody is your contact. This is no time to play around with semantics. Getting jobs in theatre involves getting people to know you and know your work. These are your contacts, and if you are good enough, and develop enough of them, one of them will pay off for you. And then it does not matter if you got introduced because he was your uncle's cousin or your drama teacher's drama teacher. He saw you, he liked you, and he hired you. How else did you expect it to happen?

The fact is that most hiring in the theatre and film world is done among acquaintances and friends: not *all* of it, but *most* of it. Obviously directors prefer to work with actors they have used before more than those they have never seen, all else being equal—and most of the time all else *is* equal. Similarly, most producers and casting directors are difficult to attract to showcase productions when total strangers are inviting them. If a producer knows you, he is more apt to drive to New Milford or Burbank Community Theatre to see you perform, and that means he is more likely to hire you.

And now, who said you have no contacts? Everybody you know is a potential contact. The actor in the community play with you might next year be producing a film; your college drama instructor might be directing a play; your uncle might have a friend who has just written a TV show. It is to your advantage to get to know people in the business; who knows what they might be doing in a month or so? Acquaintances of ours mail postcards to everyone they know every four or six months, just to stay in touch. It is not presumptuous: it is appreciated, and they get work.

The important contacts you presumably do not know yet, but you will. Every time you audition you meet at least one. At every interview you meet secretaries and other actors. These meetings can be forgotten in an instant, but if you are personable and they are intrigued by you, a contact is made. A word of caution: don't be pushy. Phony friendliness and phony friends are the most loathsome aspect of show business, and it is easy to completely misplay your hand in this way. Theatre people are the worst name-droppers in the world, and "Oh, he's a good friend of mine," becomes a line that is too frequently applied to a person met once five years ago. But you can build your real contacts—the people who know you and know your work—by simply and modestly finding ways to keep them aware of you. And you can keep aware of *them,* by writing down the name of everyone you meet in a little black book so that the next time you see them you can remember their names and what they do.

Remember these principles about contacts:

No one contact is going to make it for you, and the fact that somebody else knows somebody important is not going to make it for *him,* either. All the people you know can help you—and themselves—by trading information, tips, advice, and ultimately, offers of employment.

People you have known for years and who have subsequently "made it" may not help you out at all. That is not just because success has made them indifferent to their old pals. Many genuinely try to follow the suggestion of Edith Piaf, who said that when you reach the top you should throw the ladder back down for everybody else. But your newly arrived friends are not as secure as they seem. In fact, they are in a particularly vulnerable position. Even if they can help you they may not want to risk suggesting you to *their* superior, fearing that if you fail, they may fall. Beyond this, they may question their earlier evaluation of you now that they have new surroundings and a new perspective. They would rather you made it on your own: then they could be *sure.* This is small comfort, of course, but you will probably have to live with it.

Contacts may not look like contracts. The mousey-looking man hanging around backstage might just be getting ready to film *Cymbeline* in Portuguese, and is looking you over for the lead. Be yourself and make friends; it cannot hurt you.

Contacts may not act like contacts. People who give out jobs in show business are so besieged they frequently hide the fact behind a veil of feigned clumsiness and innocence. Play along.

All kinds of people will *tell you* that they are contacts. They're probably not. Maybe they are just nice and want to help, and maybe they are after your body. Some just like to sound important. Treat everybody the same, and do not be too sure of anyone.

A word about sleeping with the producer. If you are a talented, personable, with-it, sexy person there will be all sorts of people anxious to cast you. There will also be all sorts of people interested in going to bed with you. They may not be the same people, however. Undoubtedly several will want to cast you *and* sleep with you, and several more will want nothing to do with you. There seems to be little correlation.

A cartoon hanging outside the Screen Gems casting office window shows a young girl dressing in a bedroom and calling to an older man, "Now, when are you going to make me a star?" The older man is in the next room, smiling and cutting her a paper star.

Now it is illogical to presume that if the casting director is your steady boy friend he won't be working a little harder for you than for the average girl who comes in for a thirty-second interview. But it is equally illogical to presume that you can get an acting job merely by going from one studio bed to another. No producer makes that kind of deal; there is just too much money at stake, and too many people ready to axe *him* if you are not good enough for the role. If you go to bed with anybody, don't expect anything but a good time. In fact, a fairly thorough and empirical examination of the Hollywood/New York scene shows that the old cliché about the casting couch is now about as accurate as Ptolemaic astronomy. A young, uninhibited, and absolutely beautiful actress of our acquaintance has gone out on more than seventy-five interviews in the past ten months without even the slightest suggestion of a pass made at her. Naturally there's a lot of sexual politics to play, and many business propositions seem to have sexual implications. There are many producers who are delighted to enjoy the benefits of personal power in an industry so over-supplied with beautiful young people. (One casting director recently resigned, he said, because he was tired of pimping for his producer.) But this is all peripheral to real casting decisions. A blatant offering of your body will probably get you some takers, but it will not land you a job. In fact it might really get in your way. The young actress above relates that one of her competitors at a screen test came dressed in a micro-miniskirt and no underwear, and prominently displayed herself at the first opportunity. Not only did she fail to get the part (our friend got it) but the director kicked her off the set before the test began.

Commitment and will to succeed

This is your power supply. It keeps you going despite the thousand and one ego reversals you are bound to encounter; it keeps you going through poverty and loneliness, when your friends are marrying and having kids and making money and you are eating out of cans on the Lower East Side waiting for your ship to come in. You must continue to stay in there, to train yourself, to get information and develop contacts, to do all the things you must. In order to do all these things, you must have an overwhelming desire for success. It is often said that the people who make it in the theatre are simply those who want it badly enough.

It is not necessary to step on other people's toes, to do zany things that draw attention to yourself, or to alienate friends, relatives, and competitors in your quest for success. But quest for it you must. Getting started in theatre means *initiating* actions: getting on the telephone and on the pavement, looking up people, calling on strangers, getting to places at 6 a.m. and waiting around for three hours—all sorts of indelicate and unappetizing tasks. It also means weeks, months, even years of frustration, failure, defeat, and simple boredom. It means sitting around waiting for the telephone to ring when it has not rung in months. These things are at best unpleasant and at worst lead you to brink of suicidal depression. Only a massive will to succeed will overcome this. The commitment must be strong, persistent, and all-encompassing. All sorts of personal sacrifices simply must be assumed.

Nobody knows how long it will take to "make" you an actor. It is best to set yourself some sort of time schedule—most actors do. Three years is an average allotment: three years after the first day that you say to yourself, "I am now an actor, and I'm available for work." Three years from the day you hit the pavements, the studios, the agencies—from the day you decide that whatever you are doing, you will drop it to get the first job.

From that first day on, your commitment to your career must come first. If you are married, your spouse had better understand, or you are in trouble. If you are in college you had better be ready to drop out. If you have a job, you had better be ready—and able—to resign. For the next three years—or whatever period you set for yourself—you are going for it, and you will do what is necessary to get it.

From that day on, you scrimp on money for gifts, for food, for furniture, for an apartment. You spend money on pictures, a telephone service, résumés, classes, and some good clothes for auditions. You get the sleep you need and the medication you need; you're going to have to be ready to look terrific on an hour's notice any day of the week. You direct your time, your money, and your energy to two things: learning acting and getting work, and whatever is left over goes to less important things like your social life or your marriage. You will not always like this, of course, but if you do not do it you will fall behind. When the odds are stacked against you to begin with, who can afford to fall? If you aren't 100 percent committed, you will simply lose the job to someone who is.

A committed attitude carries with it something more than a pragmatic advantage in selling yourself on the job market. Exciting people are committed people, in art, in politics, or in life. And it is to your advantage to be exciting. So be dedicated; it will offend the weak, but it will inspire others. A life of dedication (to your art, hopefully, but even to yourself) is fulfilling; it galvanizes your talents and directs your energies. It characterizes all great artists of all times. As Bernard Shaw wrote:

"This is the true joy in life, the being used for a purpose recognized by yourself as a mighty one: the being thoroughly worn out before you are thrown on the scrap heap, the being a force of Nature instead of a feverish selfish little clod of ailments and grievances, complaining that the world will not devote itself to making you happy."

So live as if you mean it, and become an artist in the same way. This involves a little presumptuous egotism; flow with it. Michelangelo, Beethoven, Bernhardt, Heifetz, Toscannini, Aeschylus: all great artists have been persons of great dedication and temperament, persons who have sacrificed likability and pleasantness to the drive for perfection that has welled up inside them. If you are determined to "make it" as an actor, you are living life at high stakes anyway. You might as well go all the way with it.

Attitude and capacity
for psychological adjustment

How crippling is the comment, "He has a bad attitude!" It keeps talented performers out of work and gets them a place on an informal, rumor-fed blacklist which they may not truly deserve. The slightest whisper, from one associate producer to another, that "we've got enough problems in this show without dealing with *hers!*" is frequently the last exchange before "Thanks very much, dear. We'll be in touch with you if anything comes up."

It may be desirable to be daffy, but it is death to be genuinely crazy —or have producers think you are. Crazy people are hard to contract, do not show up on time, forget their lines and their blocking, annoy other actors, antagonize directors, defy wardrobers, and in general are far more trouble than they are worth. If you are crazy, hide it. If you are not, do not pretend that you are.

But mental health means more than merely being on the near side of psychosis. To be relatively stable, well-balanced, gregarious, and sensitive to the plights of others is a valuable asset. But there are more specific ways in which your attitude can work for you or against you.

Perhaps the worst attitude—tne most destructive one—that appears commonly in young actors is the one that says, "I'm waiting to be discovered." This is a complex neurosis, and its effects are virtually fatal. The actor with this attitude is afraid of trying, afraid of looking foolish, afraid of failing. He never contacts agents, never sets up interviews, and never discusses his career or his goals with anyone but close friends. He considers it callous to promote himself, and so dedicates his time to perfecting some small aspect of his craft. Secretly, he hopes that some unknown benefactor will find him in his hidden place of work and sign him to a giant film contract. But he will never take the initiative, because, he says, that would soil his purity.

One must beware of this attitude because it masks itself under seemingly noble forms. Basically it is simple fear and laziness. It is also egotism: the belief that one's own talent is so obvious that it need only be seen once to be instantly appreciated and called into demand. It is also romanticism: no Hollywood movie about the birth of a star has ever shown the aspirant plowing through the yellow pages or passing hours in the waiting rooms of an agent's office: the heroine has been discovered by the producer who visits the little summer stock theatre, or has been the understudy who is called on at the last moment to replace the aging star. The fact is that it takes plain *work* to get work in return, and *you* must go out and do it, because nobody is going to do it for you.

Another attitude that will hurt you if you overplay it is obvious disdain for the role, play, or medium for which you are auditioning. For example, it is not hard to find dozens of people working on a television series who grumble about its lack of artistic integrity. Be careful about jumping on this bandwagon. Most persons working in the theatre, films, or television like what they are doing, at least while they're doing it. At the very least they persuade themselves they like doing it. You may never watch a TV show yourself, but if you are reading for the *Andy Griffith Show* it will not help you to take a superior attitude to television or to Andy Griffith. The producers, directors, and actors are intelligent, sensitive people. They probably have pride in what they are doing, even if they do not act like it. To mock the show is to mock them, so don't be led into following their self-deprecating remarks. Every director would prefer to cast an actor who will appreciate the role, the play, and the medium.

Discipline is a primary ingredient in the professional actor's attitude. In fact, discipline is usually considered the chief distinction between the amateur and the professional. *Good* colleges, commercial schools, and community theatres insist on it, but these are in a minority. Discipline means that for the entire period between your first call and your dismissal you are concentrating on your tasks as an actor to the exclusion of everthing else. It means you are always on time: *not just usually, but always.* (There is absolutely no reason for an actor to be even one minute late to a single audition, rehearsal, or make-up call.) It means you are always prompt and ready to do what you are asked, and that all your acting instruments — voice, body, imagination, and intelligence — are at the disposal of the director every moment you are on call.

It is not always easy to see this at work in a professional situation. If you watch, for example, the taping of *Laugh-In*, you will see actors lounging around, talking to each other, joking on the set, drinking coffee, dropping lines during takes, and generally exhibiting an air of nonchalance. What you must also watch for, however, is the immediate attention that the director can command, and how within a matter of five seconds seventy-five people can snap into total concentration and readiness. The nonchalance is necessary relaxation, but it is superficial. These are professionals, conditioned like flight crews to an ever-ready professional alertness. Until you are experienced enough to have one eye always open to the job at hand, concentrate fully on what you are doing. If you do not, you might find yourself still laughing at some joke by the coffe pot while everbody else has suddenly reappeared on the set and the director is calling your name. Angrily.

Artistic temperament can be a drive for perfection and an impatience with inefficiency, or it can mask your inexperience and demonstrate your lack of discipline. It's obviously to your advantage to be easy to work with. Discipline includes a willingness to take direction. No good director will become offended or irritated by genuine questions or discussion about blocking, emphasis, or motivation, but continual complaints such as "It doesn't feel right," particularly when they are obviously meant to cover insecurity, drive directors up walls and may land you out of work. Among professionals, an inability to take direction may become your most talked-about liability, and unless you are sure that your presence in the play or film will draw thousands of paying spectators, you cannot afford that reputation.

The major cliché in director/actor hassles may be mentioned here, although if you have been in any theatre in America you have probably already heard it. That is when the "old school" director (say, George Abbot) tells the "method" actor (say, Marlon Brando) to cross left, and the actor mulls it over and asks, "What's my motivation?" "Your paycheck!" retorts the director. Nothing in today's theatre is that cut and dried, however. The actor-director relationship must be a balanced one, and both parties must genuinely desire to work well together for it to succeed. Obviously, since you are the one who is starting out, you have to do your part and a little bit more, despite possible disagreements.

In short, your attitude should be positive and infectious. You like the part, you like the play, you like the medium, you like the director and his direction, and you want like hell to do it and do it well. Nobody ever really gets offended at an actor who is genuinely eager, unless that eagerness pushes everybody else off the set. No director is offended by an actor who takes it upon himself to read the play being cast beforehand and to prepare an audition for it, or who communicates the genuine feeling that he will work like crazy if he gets the part. While you must never cross over the line by noisily and obsequiously flattering the producers, a certain touch of enthusiasm for the project is bound to be in your favor, and an overall weariness or indifference to it will work against you.

Freedom from entanglements and inhibitions

Freedom is a complex quality and it does not exist in the absolute. Everyone is bound by restraints — practical, financial, social, and mental. Success in the pursuit of an acting career involves minimizing these.

On the first level, an actor must be free to audition for roles and to accept employment when and where offered. The important job offer can come at awkward time (in the archetypal Hollywood story it always comes as the girl is about to leave on her honeymoon) and can send you to an inconvenient location. You must be free to accept it, however.

On a second level, your commitment to an acting career means a frequent (or at least occasional) slacking-off on other commitments; particulary those to husbands or wives, babies, friends, non-theatre employers, and teachers. Obviously it is better if you can arrange your priority of commitments in such a way that your career plans may proceed unhindered.

Naturally there will be some conflicts of interest here. You are an actor, but you are also a human being in a society, and you have friends, lovers, family and all sorts of people whose plans and whose feelings will affect yours. After all, there are 8760 hours in a year, and even a fully employed actor will spend 7000 of them away from the set; if you have alienated all your friends just to be at the beck and call of every agent and producer in the business, you are apt to spend a lot of lonely hours by the TV set.

The only thing you can do is to come completely to grips with the nature of the business you are trying to enter and make certain that people who may depend on you are aware of it, too, and sympathetic to your ambitions. They may not be. Many men, for example, have presented the classic ultimatum to would-be fiancees: "I'll marry you if you leave the theatre." And amazingly, many of these men are actors themselves! It is easy to condemn this attitude, but there is one thing you must recognize. If you are starting an acting career, you are not going to be the model wife or husband you learned about in home economics class or even in Masters and Johnson. You will be subject to an ever-changing, unpredictable schedule, you will be on call for location work in Yugoslavia or New Haven while your spouse is taking care of the house and babies, you will be facing the terrific frustration of looking for parts and breaks in an industry where unemployment is routine and finally, when you start to get work, you will be deeply involved in the emotional crises, love affairs, and strange psychologies of the characters you are given to play. All of this, frankly, can prove incompatible with a happy home life, and the actor or actress must fully prepare himself and his potential spouse for the trials their relationship will inevitably face.

Should an actor get married at all? Well, it is far beyond the scope of this little book to recommend one way or the other, and it is also doubtful if any recommendation here would be very seriously considered anyway. However, it is obvious that marriage *can* become a serious entanglement to a stage or film career if both partners fail to understand what they are getting into. The actor who marries without such understanding either completely frustrates his spouse, and the marriage ends up in ruins, or he frustrates himself, and *he* ends up in ruins. The fact that the acting profession has a ridiculously high divorce rate is one of which you are already aware.

Marriage is also a serious entanglement to a young actor if it puts major financial limitations on his career. A young man with a family to support is hardly in a position to spend great portions of his money on photographs, and great portions of his time on unremunerative occupations such as pavement-pounding and waiting-room waiting. If two young actors marry, one may have to get a "regular job" in order to support the other's career, and this can breed resentment.

Ideally a young actor should only marry if he is rich or working, or marrying somebody who is. And he should only marry someone who understands the rigors of the career. Having said this we rest our case. There are, after all, more than pragmatic considerations in this matter.

There are other entanglements besides marriage, of course. Some are financial, some emotional. You may be unwilling or unable to move around, to work with certain kinds of people, or to play certain kinds of parts. You may object to undressing in front of a camera (or an audience) or performing behavior you find undignified. There is a line you must draw for yourself here, but naturally the lower that line (i.e, the fewer your inhibitions) the more "available" you are. Insofar as that line now must be drawn to include or exclude doing nude scenes (which exist in almost all movies) you will have to be prepared to define your views on this if you plan to work in films. There is, however, one "inhibition" which is known as "taste." An actor *must* be inhibited from doing things that are tasteless and unrewarding. Performing in the nude for an Antonioni film and for a one-day stag movie obviously have different values, both as art and as a step in your professional career. A boy or girl who is 100 percent available and uninhibited for a blue film and a $25 fee may find himself unusable for anything *but* that in the future.

Good information and advice

Finally, you need the best current information and advice if you are to pursue a career successfully. This book may be filled with good advice, but it is not enough. You need to know the day-by-day developments in your medium.

Both the theatre and film worlds have their trade journals, which report such developments. In Hollywood these are the *Hollywood Reporter* and *Daily Variety*, published daily during the week and with an annual anniversary issue. In New York they are *Show Business* and *Backstage*, published weekly. In addition, the New York weekly *Variety* provides world-wide coverage of all entertainment media. *Variety* is roughly ten times the size of the others. The usefulness of reading the trades is not immediately obvious. Generally they contain information more valuable to producers than aspiring actors. *Backstage* and *Show Business* (as well as the weekly *Variety*) carry casting columns, but the information is not always current and correct, and important auditions are not always listed. The Hollywood trade papers do not even list casting calls except on very rare occasions; these occur when a studio needs certain types of people badly enough to advertise in the trades. If you live in Los Angeles and subscribe to *Daily Variety*, you may find yourself reading merely who has been cast in what, and who is selling a house in Malibu for $250,000.

On the other hand, it is very much to your advantage to subscribe to the trade papers, or at least to read them from time to time. For one thing, they *are* the most current reports on what is happening in your business. Even if the information is not particularly relevant to your immediate interest (getting work), it will give you a basic understanding of what is going on. It will let you know what is on the minds of agents, producers, and casting directors, and give you a vocabulary of names, places, and shows being done in your area. Both papers regularly list the names of agents, casting directors, and people you should try to know, and you can at least start to become familiar with who they are in case you meet them. Futher, reading the papers gives you a vicarious sense of participation in the business even if you have not really started out, and it will help you overcome your naturally alien feelings.

Where else do you get information? Talk to people. Actors love to talk about their business. Acting schools, theatre bars, and off-off-Broadway (in New York and Los Angeles) showings are natural places to make the acquaintance of other actors and to trade information and tips. Get as many ideas and opinions as you can; beware of being overly influenced by any single person's likes, dislikes, neuroses, or phobias. Gradually you will gain a working knowledge of what casting possibilities are hot, which agents are really working for which actors, which producers are open to what kinds of suggestions, and in general what your competition is likely to be.

There are theatre schools that specialize in teaching you "how to audition" and "how to get a job," as well as "how to act." They may be useful. There are also public lectures on these subjects from time to time; they are usually advertised in trade magazines. Of course there are always a lot of people willing to take your money in return for "inside" tips and suggestions. With these people you begin to reach the point of diminishing returns, however. No matter how much you may read or hear about the subject of "making it" in acting, nothing begins to approach the knowledge you get by working toward success yourself. The best way to learn the business is to get started, to participate. The suggestions in the rest of the book will indicate some ways to do it. Once you get your start, you can leave this book behind. You will be finding information much more specifically applicable to your needs.

Luck

Luck is placed last on this list, simply because there is nothing you can do to get it. Luck is a factor that can outweigh most of the rest, and there is nothing to do about it but groan.

In the British theatre, acting success can be achieved merely by ascending a very well-defined ladder. If you are good enough (as proven by audition) to gain admission to the Royal Academy of Dramatic Art (or any of the top six drama schools in London), and good enough to stay in through graduation, you are virtually assured employment at one of the many regional repertory companies in the British Isles. From there it is simply a matter of perfecting your craft, and "working up" to one of the prestigious companies, the National Theatre and the Royal Shakespeare Company being at the top of the heap. If you become a leading performer at one of the leading companies, you will most probably be offered film roles. British actors tend to be a lot less neurotic than their American counterparts, since the steps to a career are so clearly laid out.

In America luck is much more important, particularly in film acting. Witness Shelly Duvall, the young starlet of *Brewster McCloud* and *McCabe and Mrs. Miller*. Miss Duvall, at the time she was cast in *Brewster*, had never studied acting, had never seen a play, and generally disdained theatre people as "weird." She was a suburban housewife living in Houston, Texas, and she was "discovered" while selling her husband's paintings to people who turned out to be MGM producers. The dream of "discovery" lies deep in the heart of every aspiring performer, but it comes almost as often to those who do not work for it as to those who do. Shirley MacLaine was "discovered" when she was called upon to substitute for Carol Haney in the Broadway musical, *Pajama Game*. Hal Wallis was in the audience, and but for that occurrence, Miss MacLaine might still be hoofing on 45th Street. It also turns out that MacLaine was planning to resign from the show the very night that Haney turned her ankle. But what do *you* do about luck? You don't go to Houston to sell oil paintings; that's for sure. You will have to find your own.

○○○○○○○○○○○○○○○○○○○○○○
○   ○
○   THREE   ○
○   ○
○○○○○○○○○○○○○○○○○○○○○○

WHAT DO YOU DO NOW?

Well, we now assume that you are convinced you have talent, and are prepared to make a career. You are going to look for work, so what do you do now?

Your medium

The three theatrical media are stage, film and broadcasting (which for all practical purposes means television). Allied media in which you may find employment are variety and nightclub work and modeling, but we shall limit our concern to the three acting media. These are divided into subgroups. Included in professional stage work are Broadway and off-Broadway shows, summer stock and regional repertory companies, industrial productions, and guest-artist stints at drama schools and universities. Included in film are feature films and documentaries. In television there are filmed and taped specials, series shows, commercials, and live announcing positions. Since television makes great use of filmed programming, the two media are virtually inseparable, from the actor's point of view, and no real choice need be made between them at the early stages of a career. Your major decision, then, is between stage and camera work.

You should first seek advice from your teachers and valued critic/ friends on the medium to which you may best be suited. In weighing the alternatives open to you, the following points should be taken into consideration.

Stage work demands great versatility and projection. Stage actors are called upon to do a wide variety of roles, frequently before a thousand or more people at one sitting. A strong, penetrating voice capable of great subtlety is an absolute necessity. You should have a face that projects emotion without mugging, a body that moves well, and a personality that without pushing carries well beyond the footlights. Similarly, you should have a command of verse-speaking and classical acting styles, because most stage careers begin in theatres which produce classical plays. Strong talents in the areas of music and dance are valuable to the stage actor, though not absolutely necessary. Above all, the stage actor needs the great intangibles: talent, presence, and timing. He must be able to enunciate subtle nuances to huge audiences without looking as if he is reading from a speech textbook, and he must convey the sense of a vibrant personality whether he is playing hero, villain, or village idiot.

If your talents lie, on the other hand, in the area of extremely naturalistic performing, a film or television career is probably more suitable. Acting before a camera ruthlessly shows up all but the most honest of performers. It virtually obviates the need for projection, since the camera and microphone can be placed inches away. It is frequently said that the film actor is the pawn of the director, cameraman, editor, and sound mixer. "The cameraman usurps the actor's physical composition, the sound mixer his intonation, and the editor his timing," according to one highly successful stage and film actor. Thus, for the camera actor it is personality, looks, "quality," and honesty which become premium qualifications.

In general a person's looks count less for him in live theatre than in camera theatre, mainly because make-up can do much more at fifty feet than in a larger-than-life film close-up. Many persons who are genuinely plain have had brilliant stage careers but have found it impossible to get work in Hollywood. By contrast, a person who is astonishingly beautiful or interesting in a unique way can begin to get film work almost on that basis alone.

Your home base

One more element to consider is where you want to live. As an actor you really only have three choices: you can live in New York, you can live in Hollywood, or you can live somewhere on the LORT circuit. These choices involve different kinds of theatrical activity and different life styles and business procedures for you.

The LORT circuit

The LORT circuit is comprised of those theatres associated in the League of Resident Theatres. They are union theatres producing full seasons of plays in various cities in America and Canada, such as Washington, D.C., Louisville, Seattle, San Francisco, Minneapolis, and Cleveland. A more complete list is given in the appendix. There are over thirty such theatres, and many have fine, permanent homes. Their artistic work is reviewed constantly in trade papers and scholarly journals, as well as in the local presses. An excellent book, regularly revised, describes many of them in detail; this is Julius Novick's *Beyond Broadway* (Hill and Wang, 1968).

If you are a college senior or recent graduate, you will have a marvelous opportunity to contract with a LORT theatre by attending the Chicago auditions sponsored by the Theatre Communications Group (TCG) previously mentioned. TCG is an autonomous, non-profit organization operated with funds from the Ford Foundation; it seeks to coordinate the activities (particularly casting) of the LORT theatres. Each fall TCG writes to the drama department heads at all US colleges. These department heads (usually in consultation with their faculties) nominate about 500 students, who must be seniors or graduates from the past two years. These students audition at regional centers before TCG representatives in January. The regional centers are Los Angeles, New York, San Francisco, Seattle, Chicago, St. Louis, Austin, Cincinnati, Washington, Detroit, Atlanta, and Boston. From these regional qualifying auditions about eighty candidates are invited to final auditions in Chicago. These are held in March, and to them come the artistic directors and company managers of virtually all the LORT companies. According to TCG officials, about half of the auditioners are offered "immediate employment" (i.e., beginning the following September). Generally these actors receive Equity contracts for a minimum of one season.

Unfortunately you cannot get to the Chicago auditions without first qualifying in the regional auditions, and you cannot get into the qualification round without a nomination from the head of your drama department. If your department does not nominate you, there is nothing you can do via TCG, and you should not try. Every year students not nominated show up in Chicago hoping to get an audition squeezed in because of a no-show. It never happens. "Absolutely and unequivocally not," say the directors of TCG. But remember, if you are not nominated by your department upon graduation, you still have two years of eligibility, and even though you may not apply directly for a nomination, it would not be considered unwise or presumptuous, in most cases, to make your interest in a nomination known to the proper people.

The TCG-sponsored auditions are not the only means of applying for admission to the resident companies, although they are the best way. There are also the University Resident Theatre Association (URTA) auditions, held during January and February in Chicago, New York, Memphis, and San Francisco. The URTA auditions are viewed by the directors of about twenty URTA member companies; however the "jobs" offered are almost invariably graduate student assistantships with stipends (of around $1500-$3000 per year) for teaching instead of salaries for acting. URTA theatres are all based in colleges and universities, even though a few are Equity companies.*

You may, of course, write directly to a resident theatre in which you are interested and request an audition. Most companies have general auditions once or twice a year (some more frequently than that) and a

*If you are interested in pursuing the URTA audition route, write to Robert C. Schnitzer, Director, URTA, Mendelssohn Theatre, Ann Arbor, Michigan 48108. Current URTA members are Bowling Green State University, Brigham Young University, Florida State University, Illinois State University, Louisiana State University, Memphis State University, Michigan State University, Pennsylvania State University, Wayne State University, Harvard University, the Universities of Colorado, Denver, Indiana, Michigan, Minnesota, Missouri (Columbia), Missouri (Kansas City), Nebraska, Northern Colorado, Pennsylvania and Utah, and Stephens College. As with the TCG auditions, a student must be nominated by the head of his undergraduate department, but unlike TCG, URTA does not solicit nominations; it is up to the student to initiate the nomination.

letter to them with a picture and a résumé might stimulate a response. For that matter, nothing prevents you from showing up at the theatre's stage door and requesting an audition or at least an appointment with the company's artistic director. If you have a contact with the company this could be arranged fairly easily. Even if you do not and you chance to come at a convenient time, you may get in for a hearing. But you must not really expect anything to come of it. The director may enjoy the diversion, but he is highly unlikely to really be looking for someone like you at the moment you pass by, and it is very doubtful that anything will come of your effort. There are easier methods of getting work than driving around the LORT circuit looking for ways to break into it.

Acting on the LORT circuit is considered an ideal way of life by many of the actors engaged in it. Some extraordinarily good actors make most or all of their living working with these regional repertory companies, and some of America's finest stage productions have come from this circuit. The work is fairly steady (at least, the contracts are for a season and not for the run of any given play), the pay is decent, and the chance to work with several directors on several challenging roles is one that actors cherish. Moreover the experience is generally transferable, and one LORT job can easily lead to another once you get a good reputation among the LORT directors. And who knows when your LORT production will go to Broadway (as *The Great White Hope* did)?

New York and Hollywood

If you are not auditioning in Chicago and are not headed for a LORT theatre general audition, or are not interested in the LORT scene to begin with, you will be headed for New York or Hollywood. Nowhere else, really. Virtually all live professional theatre is cast in New York — even LORT productions are generally cast there. TCG, for example, has audition facilities for the year round use of LORT directors who come to town for that purpose. Summer stock casts in New York, as do industrial shows, dinner shows, and touring shows. Even Los Angeles producers of live theatre do much of their casting in New York (much to the dismay and fury of local actors). Conversely, most film features, all filmed network television, and much live TV are cast in Hollywood, and many of the programs and films are made there, too. If you are a stage actor, you should go to New York. If camera is your medium, go West. Go, in any case, where your share of the action is likely to be.

As cities, New York and Hollywood are as unalike as Paris and Peking. New York is a filthy town which is either loved and hated by everyone who comes in contact with it. The old chestnut, "New York's a great place to visit, but I wouldn't want to live there," has never been truer than today. "Fun City" is beset with urban ills which make most of those anywhere else seem, in scale, as bothersome as a few broken street lights. The city is grimy, overpriced, over-robbed, over-mugged, and riddled with dope addiction, racial and religious chaos, broken-down transportation, bitter people, a bad climate, and a general feeling of futility. Despite all this there are those who love New York, those to whom the prospect of crossing over the Hudson River into the city sends chills up and down the spine. New York for all its faults, is at the very pulse of America, and there is a feeling about living in the midst of that power that makes anywhere else seem "hick."

Los Angeles is blessed with a fairer climate but cursed with a miserably polluted atmosphere, nonexistent public transportation, a crazy city layout that has virtually no downtown area, lethargic people, a generally anti-cultural atmosphere, and an unstable populace that moves in and out at a rate of nearly 5000 people a week. There is almost nothing exciting about Los Angeles itself; there are virtually no public places where actors congregate without an invitation, and exclusivity imposes a special kind of remoteness which the young actor may find his way out of. You can become part of the New York "scene" in a matter of weeks, but you may live in Los Angeles for years without even finding a Hollywood equivalent to it. Even telephoning someone across town results in a toll charge, and getting to his house without your own car takes half a day. These factors themselves may help you make up your mind. After all, it is not just your career, it is your whole life that is up for grabs; and you ought to decide what kinds of environmental problems you are best at facing.

Jumping media

Actors are frequently advised to go to New York to build up credits before coming to Hollywood. This implies a great interchange between media and a certain ease in jumping from one to the other. It is certainly true that among the finest new male film actors are a number who began their careers in live theatre in New York; these are Stacy Keach, Jr., Frank Langella, Dustin Hoffman, Alan Arkin, and others like them. Yet these men had reached virtually "star" status in New York (at least off-Broadway) before the film industry began to notice them. Few women make the jump at all. Colleen Dewhurst, a superb New York actress with credits and awards three blocks long, admits, when asked why she has done only two small film roles in her career, "It's because nobody's asked me." And as the sometime wife of George C. Scott, she does not lack contacts.

The truth is that it is very difficult to transfer credits from New York to Hollywood as you would, for example, from one graduate school to another. Minor credits in one town are almost worthless as stepping stones in the other; they can even be a hindrance among Hollywood producers highly suspicious of "arty" off-Broadway and Broadway performers. New York actors come to Hollywood and moan, "They've never heard of me!" even though they may have major, man-on-the-street reputations back home. "Off-Broadway auditions for Broadway, which auditions for Hollywood," says veteran multi-media performer James Coco, but Coco's own career attests that Hollywood only pays attention to those who first rise to the top in the East.

Part of the difficulty in jumping from one medium to another is that few actors are equally adept at both. The different qualities mentioned earlier (projection versus intimacy) apply not just at the beginning of an actor's career, but all the way through. Most actors, truthfully, are not universally accomplished; producers have frequently despaired after casting a film star in a stage lead or vice versa. Another difficulty is simply the ignorance which most Hollywood directors and producers have of New York theatre. New York is, after all, 2500 miles distant, and film people on a trip East aren't eager to probe Greenwich Village for discoveries. Frank Langella, for example, had won numerous off-Broadway awards, had played several seasons of summer stock, and had performed a leading role at New York's Lincoln Center long before he was tapped for his first film role. The same is true of virtually everyone who has successfully jumped from the stage to the screen.

So it is folly to assume, as many do, that the young actor can spend a couple of years in New York to "get exposure" and then head for Hollywood with credits under his arm. He will have only a suitcase under his arm, and he will have to start all over. The best suggestion we can make is to decide which medium you will be best at, now, next year, and three years from now, and head for the proper geographical center.

Establishing yourself

You have moved, then, to your new city. The first thing you must do is to *establish* yourself. Obviously you need a place to stay. If you are going to New York, and you have not been there before, prepare yourself: you simply will not *believe* what you are asked to pay for the dingiest apartment or hotel room imaginable. If possible, move in with a friend and give yourself a couple of weeks to look for a rent-controlled apartment in a decent area; better yet, move to New York with a friend or two and share a place and the rent among you. Bring enough money to pay two months' rent in advance plus a deposit, plus a few hundred dollars in reserve. If you head for Los Angeles, you can expect to find a more reasonably priced place to stay. What is more, it will be cleaner and nicer to come home to; the limitation there is you absolutely must have a car in good running condition.

Once you are settled, you can get to work. There will be many things you need. There is no particular order in which you should get them, but you should get them fast. These are:

> A dependable source of income
> A telephone and a telephone service
> Pictures of yourself
> A résumé of your training and experience
> Colleagues
> Up-to-date information
> An agent

A dependable source of income

Obviously you need this. You simply cannot pay your bills, eat, dress, or go out into the world without money. Moreover, you cannot afford to scrimp on professional expenses like photographs and classes. Perhaps you have regular income from home, or from your working husband, or from an indulgent lover. That is magnificent and you need not worry so long as your source continues to take care of you, though generally something is expected in return. If you are not so lucky, you will have to get a job, and preferably one with flexible hours that pays well. In Hollywood, since most work and interviews are done in the daytime, an evening job (say, as a waiter or waitress) is ideal. In New York the same is true until you start to perform or work at night in off-off-Broadway. Many actors work graveyard shifts in New York to be available during all "normal" hours. The back pages of trade journals frequently advertise part-time jobs particularly suitable to the personalities and strange schedules of aspiring actors.

One agent recommends that anyone coming to New York or Hollywood first prepare himself or herself with a salable skill, and he goes on to suggest office skills — stenography and typing — as ideal ones. Why? Financial solvency is so vitally important. It may take three to five years before you even know *if* you're ever going to make money in sufficient quantities to live, and in bad times unskilled odd jobs are scarcer than acting jobs. At least a secretary works and eats, and if you land the right kind of job in a theatre-related area, you start to get contacts while you work. There are many girls and boys (male secretaries are now commonplace in Hollywood and becoming so in New York) who have started in the office and ended up on stage. Anything — hairdressing, bartending, housepainting — is better in the long run than making porny films for hack photographers on Sunset Boulevard.

A telephone and telephone service

These are both musts. You must be reachable in order to get any work at all, and nobody in New York or Los Angeles relies on the mail service for this. A telephone will cost you anywhere from $6.00 to $10.00 a month (plus long distance charges) and is a virtual necessity. There will be times when you do not want to stay home and wait for it to ring, so you need a telephone service, too. The service either answers your phone for you when you are out (via an electronic hookup), or takes messages for you at another number when you cannot be reached at yours. The first service is apt to cost about $20 a month, and while it is preferable due to its simplicity (you need only give out one number to agents and producers), the "if no answer" service is much cheaper (as low as $3 monthly) and just as effective. In either case you soon get in the habit of calling your service whenever you get home to see if there are any messages for you, and you face the discouragement of hearing the bright voice on the other end gaily declare, "No messages today!" or "All clear!" If you pale at the thought of continually calling your service and getting the inevitably discouraging results, or if you have a good sum of money to invest in a long-term saving, you might buy a recording device which attaches to your telephone and answers it for you, playing your own recorded voice to your callers and recording their message for your eventual playback when you return. This device costs anywhere from $150 up, and more expensive versions can be programmed in such a way that you can call your own phone from wherever you happen to be and listen to messages that have come in since you left; it is every bit as good as a personal answering service and less expensive over a couple of years.

Photographs

These, as we have mentioned, are your calling cards. No actor can be without photographs, which are in two basic forms:

Photographs for distribution. These are mass produced and, together with your résumé, are given out to anybody who seems to have a professional reason for wanting them.

Photographs in your "book," which you carry around to interviews and auditions and show to interested directors and producers.

Of course you need both, but they can be acquired at the same time. The standard procedure is for the actor to go to a photographer and have a set of photos made; he then selects one or two to mass-duplicate, and others to go in his book. The duplications are rarely made by the photographer (who, unless he specializes in mass printing, will charge up to $2.00 apiece for them). Instead, you send them to one of the quantity reproduction laboratories in New York or Los

Angeles which print them for as low as 10¢ or 12¢ apiece. You can find excellent quantity reproduction labs listed in the yellow pages of both cities; call them for current prices.

Finding a photographer and selecting the kind of photographs you will need, however, is a much more complex process. There is great disagreement over what is desirable in the way of photographs, and you will probably experiment many times before you land a successful portfolio of photos. All should be on 8x10 glossy stock. Here are the variables:

    Formats: Single head shot
             Composite head shots
             Composite head shots plus abbreviated résumé
             Body shots
             Composite of head and body shots

    Style: Studio-posed
           Candid
    Film: 35mm
          140mm
          View camera (5" x 7", 4" x 5", or 8" x 10")

Naturally, with thousands of actors and thousands of photographers all aiming at some sort of originality, there are bound to be countless variations on the above alternatives, and some undoubtedly succeed.

The composite photograph is a laboratory print which combines two or more shots of you into a single 8" x 10" photo. Three or four poses are common, but some composites have five, six, or seven shots crammed into the 80 square inches. The idea of a composite is to show the various expressions, attitudes, and characteristics of your face and your personality. Frequently each separate shot is in a different costume, and perhaps also a different make-up. One shot is often considerably larger than the others, and becomes your "basic" look, with the other shots supporting it by showing "what else you can look like." A good composite must be done with great precision in the laboratory, so that light levels in the various shots balance each other, the lines separating the prints are straight and even, and the overall composition is effective. Often the actor's name, agent, and phone number can be printed right on the composite and his résumé printed on the back, though this is expensive.

Most producers, however (particularly in theatre and film work, as opposed to commercials), prefer the straight, full, 8″ x 10″ head shot. This is universally true in Hollywood, and about 70 percent true in New York. Why? The head shot makes a bold, single impression. The Hollywood casting director does not want to hire you for four roles, but just for one. The composite dilutes your look. Surprisingly, this also seems to be true for repertory company casting directors, who will simply assume that you can change under make-up. The principal goal of your photographs should be to show you *as you are*. That which is beautiful, dramatic, sensitive, virile, or interesting in your appearance should look as if it is coming from you rather than from some darkroom magician.

The same considerations apply to the style and format of your pictures. You should know enough of the nature of photography to make an intelligent choice here.

Studio-posed photographs are generally made with a studio or view camera. It is called a view camera because the photographer can preview his exact photograph (upside down) on a ground glass screen behind the camera. The view camera uses large film: usually 4″ x 5″ per negative and sometimes as large as 8″ x 10″. This gives him two advantages: first he can make all sorts of corrections on his negative, such as airbrushing away facial blemishes and compensating for weak features in your bone structure. Secondly, his print will be enlarged at most only four times its negative size, so that the quality will be superior, and the lighting and shading effects (as well as your skin tone) can be masterfully subtle. Also, the studio conditions allow him to light the subject (you) exquisitely and with fine attention to detail. The photographic portraits by Karsh of Ottowa, for example, use this process and are considered masterpieces.

On the other hand the studio and its camera impose huge limitations. Its very photographic superiority bespeaks a kind of staleness, a 1950's phoniness. Just as films are now made almost entirely on location instead of on a sound stage, most contemporary photographic portraiture is done outdoors under "natural light" conditions, and for the same reasons. Outdoor candid photography conveys a "with it" vitality which does not come across in posed studio photographs, no matter how good. Thirty-five millimeter film is far less expensive than the larger variety, and a photographer can take thirty-six different candid shots with the same amount of film it takes for *one* 8″ x 10″ view camera exposure. Since the 35mm camera is light and small, a photographer and subject can roam freely and easily in many locations, shooting quickly and easily without posing at all, and come home with 500 negatives to choose from. The limitation of this form of photography, of course, is that the negative must be enlarged nearly 40 times to make an 8″ x 10″ print (even more if the negative is "cropped"—i.e., if only a fraction of it is actually used) and the print quality tends to be grainy and without delicate shadings. For a dramatic and exciting photograph, however, this is not a limitation. The very graininess, according to many producers (and even photographers) is an asset (it gives a picture liveliness and a sense of movement) and the natural, unretouched look gives a photo charm and a sense of authenticity. Besides, motion picture films themselves are made on 35mm stock, so that there is little sense in previewing yourself in the larger film when they are looking for you in the smaller.

A very popular compromise in film size is 140mm film, which is used in twin-lens reflex cameras like the Rolleiflex, or the fine Swedish single-lens reflex, the Hasselblad. 140mm photography uses a negative that is 2¼″ square and produces a finer print than the 35mm, with less graininess and more subtlety. It costs a few cents more per shot. The 140mm camera is only a little larger than the 35mm and has no significant limitations.

How much should a beginning portfolio cost? There are professional photographers in New York and Los Angeles who specialize in photographing actors. Their services run anywhere from $25 to $250 and more for a session, which can vary from a single studio sitting to an all-day romp with camera in Central Park. Be sure of what you are getting.

What you need, basically, are about five to ten good shots of yourself. They should look like you do *at your best*. They should mainly be head shots and head-and-shoulder shots, though you can have one from the waist up if you wish. (*No* cheesecakes, unless you are auditioning for a Las Vegas strip show.) The photographer will take his shots and in a day or so show you proof sheets from which to make your selections. He will then print the eight or ten you select.

His fee for this will vary enormously, depending on his market value; you can pay as little as $35 for this but you will probably pay more for a good photographer. If you pay more than $100, you should have evidence that he is one of the very best, because that fee is high. You then take the best shot and have a hundred copies made for about $15. The copies should be virtually as good as the original, or you can have them redone.

Different photographers have different set-ups, of course, and may offer to sell their prints in other combinations. Some will include the mass-produced 100 copies in their price (usually they will send them to the same place you would and add twice the cost). Others charge a flat rate for the session and two final prints, and additional fees for everything else, including the making of composites. Others simply charge a sitting fee and a per print charge beyond that; this is surely the fairest way.

Frequently the photographer will offer other services as well. Some have a means of offset-printing your photograph onto regular bond paper; they can then print your résumé on the back. Composites are a standard photographic process, and your photographer will advise you on how to make up a composite from your individual proofs, if you desire one. In general the photographer will have his own ideas as to how you should be photographed and what you should have; he will also be happy to tell you which shots *he* prefers and which ones producers are likely to prefer. The trouble is that he is not really apt to know more than you do; it is simply a good business practice to act as if he does. Remember, he is not going for work, you are. His income comes from taking pictures, not acting in plays or movies. Still, his reputation comes from the actors he has photographed who have gone on to successful careers, and his advice should be listened to with attention.

There is nothing to prevent you and a friend from getting together and taking your own photographs, and though the professionals will gripe at our saying this, there's no great mystique in photography that time and care cannot master. Simply go to a camera store and rent for a day or two a good 35mm single-lens reflex camera with a through-the-lens light meter and buy half a dozen rolls of Tri-X film. The camera shop owner will be happy to explain the camera's operation, and you and your friend can go out and shoot each other all day long. The camera you will rent will take care of proper exposure; if you compose each shot well and remember to focus (these are relatively simple operations with a single-lens reflex camera, since you actually look through the actual shooting lens, not the little window you might remember from your Polaroid or Brownie), you will come home with about 100 shots of each of you, and some of them are bound to be good ones. Have the film developed and printed on contact sheets by the camera store, and then have the best negatives enlarged. For a dollar or two extra, (and maybe for free, if you are now a good friend of the camera shop owner) you can have the choicest negatives "custom printed" and they will be "cropped" (shaped) and printed with special care. On the West Coast the approximate cost of all this is as follows:

Camera rental:	$10
Film	8
Developing	3
Contact prints	6
20 prints	20
	$47

This comes out at less than $25 apiece for the two of you. If you own or can borrow a camera you save another $5 each. And if you have taken some good shots, you have not only saved money, you may get ideas about opening up a little source of side income for yourself. If, on the other hand, the contact sheets look terrible, you need not have to have them printed up and you have not lost much money.

Here are some tips on taking pictures of an actor — and on being photographed as an actor:

Take the pictures outdoors on a bright, *grey* day: never in direct sunlight, which causes harsh shadows, squinting, and washed-out skin tones.

Get close. Either use a telephoto lens (preferable for close-ups, believe it or not) or get right up to the actor's face; let the face fill at least half and preferably up to two-thirds of the frame. The less you will have to enlarge it, the better; 90 percent of all amateur photography could be improved simply by having the photographer step forward fifteen feet.

Relax the subject. Talk, joke, distract him. Have him bob his head and shoot him as he comes up. Give him things to say and do, then stop him with a word and shoot. Or shoot him without stopping him.

Take a variety of poses: smiles, laughs (genuine!), glares, thoughtful reflections, full-face stares, angled gazes, profiles. You can pick the best later.

Enjoy yourself. The advantages of doing photographs yourself is that you can spend more time just horsing around and capturing some jolly, spontaneous moods. These are quite likely to result in fine photos. You can mix in mood shots, but be prepared not to like them when you see them developed later.

Return the camera.

Résumés

The actor's résumé is a listing of the parts he has played (and where) on a single mimeographed sheet, together with such basic information as his name, height, hair color, eye color, weight, age range, and telephone number (or agent's telephone number), plus any further information that might be helpful in getting work. The sheet is mimeographed or otherwise duplicated, and attached to the photograph. Some photographers can do this as part of the printing process, but there is nothing wrong with simply stapling a résumé to the back of a photo. No actor ever got hired because of an expensive printing job on his photo-résumé, and none has ever lost a part because his data was mimeographed and not offset. Neatness is important; opulence is not.

What information should you list? As to your physical characteristics, be realistic. If you are a girl and weigh in at 150, you'd better say so or they will be mad when you show up 30 pounds heavier than what you put down. And even though you played a 96-year-old man in a college production, do not go in for odd age ranges. Generally you can give yourself a spread of five to ten years without getting into any trouble. Moreover, it helps establish your image if you specify a narrow age range or even simply give your exact age.

As to your credits, your professional experience are the only really important ones. If you have played an extra in a TV pilot, that goes above playing St. Joan in college. If you are a union member, say so on the résumé. If you are not but you have acted with a union company, put that at the top of your list. If you have acted with known stars, list them. If you have done only college or school shows, go ahead and list them blithely, and make sure you act as though they were the most important shows done in the three-state area in which you lived.

Unfortunately, a standard piece of advice is often given young actors preparing a résumé: lie. It is an even bet as to whether you are better off doing so; you can get caught lying about professional credits, and nobody really cares much about your amateur credits. At times actors have falsely listed roles in productions directed, unknown to them, by the persons to whom they were showing their résumés. The results can be guessed.

A producer once auditioned three girls, each one of whom listed the same role in the same production on her résumé. The producer in question merely smiled, knowing the practice was common. However, he also cast another girl in the part. We will not advise you to lie. However, if you understudied Hamlet at Nevada State and ran through it only in the trap room downstairs while the "real" Hamlet was performing on stage, go ahead and list it. The important thing is to list roles that you played and were good at — roles that you could play well again if you were asked.

Things which you should not include on your résumé are:

> Your interest or experience in directing
>
> Your membership in Phi Beta Kappa
>
> Your high school or college grades
>
> Your hobbies
>
> Your reasons for wanting a job
>
> Your dedication to acting
>
> Your willingness to do *anything* and *everything*
>
> Your psychological history
>
> Your marital situation

Things you might include are:

> Your special abilities (i.e., performance sports, such as high diving, which you do superbly; circus acts, singing and dance experience, nightclub work, etc.)

Your training in acting, singing, dance (listing the names of
your instructors if they are well known)
Languages you speak fluently
Accents you do fluently

Actors vary as to what they wish to put on their résumés. The controlling criterion should be what will get a producer or director interested in you. There is no particular "must" format; most agents have their own for their clients, and nobody has come up with a case for or against any one of them. If you want to include a couple of humanizing details (such as your astrological sign), you can do so at the risk of seeming "cutesy"; in general resumes should be clear and simple, and should show your experience at a glance. Don't ever think you can make up for a lack of quality in your credits by substituting quantity. Actors who cram thirty-five amateur roles onto one sheet of paper (or worse, two or three) make it clear that they have been wasting away in the boondocks longer than has been good for them. It is better to show a half-dozen credits that look interesting than five dozen that look repetitious.

Agents and agencies

No character in the theatre or film industry arouses such contradictory attitudes as the agent. To the beginning actor, without contacts and without credits, the agent is the guide to fame and fortune. Actors fall all over themselves trying to get an agent to "represent" them, to put their case over to the moguls in the executive offices, and to do their hatchet work, spade work, telephoning, and interviewing. To the established actor, by contrast, the agent is often a vampire in disguise, sucking the performer's talent and forcing him into commercial ventures devoid of artistic merit, all for 10 percent. A famous actor recently paid his agency a commission of more than $10,000 — in pennies, hauled up in an armored truck. Lawsuits and contract-breaking between actors and their agents are unfortunately common in this volatile industry.

Simply speaking, an agent is a person who makes his income by helping you make yours. The agent's job is to get you employment, and for his efforts in doing so, he takes a percentage of your salary. The percentage varies according to the medium. All filmed work performed under a Screen Actors' Guild contract authorizes the agent to take up to 10 percent, and invariably that is what the agent will take. For stage work under Equity auspices, the agent takes only a percentage of the income you make above the Equity minimum. If you are signed to a regional theatre at a union scale (minimum) wage, or even $10 a week more than that, you pay no commission. If you are paid the minimum plus $50, you pay 5 percent for the first ten weeks. If you are paid the minimum plus $150, you pay 5 percent for the first six months, and so forth. As a rule, New York agents do not make very much money representing young actors. That is why you will find that the agent's position there is much less important than in Hollywood. In any case, the agent does not make *any* money unless you do, so that it is entirely to his advantage to get you work and a good price for that work. In theory, one can hardly find fault with such a system.

Still speaking theoretically, an agent works as follows. You agree with an agent (we will discuss how you do *this* later) that he will represent you, and your agreement is formalized with a contract. Your agent will then take your pictures (which you still provide at your expense) and attach them to new résumés (which he makes up in his agency's format and at his expense). This becomes your photo-résumé, and it lists the agency telephone number and not yours as the contact for all ensuing negotiations. Your agent will then search through whatever casting information is available to him, and will send your photo-résumé to those producers who he has reason to feel are looking for someone like you. If your agent is a good one, he will be on the phone all the time with producers looking for specific types of actors or actresses to play specific parts. If you are suitable he will send your photo-résumé for the producer's examination. (These photo-résumés, by the way, are *never* returned, so you had better be prepared to give your agent an inexhaustible supply). If the producer is interested, he then calls the agent, the agent calls you, and an interview and/or audition is set up at the producer's convenience. The agent will give you whatever information he can get about the part, and if you are a particularly favored client, or he has the time and thinks it would be a good idea, he may personally escort you to the interview, introduce you to the producers, and try in other ways to grease the machinery for you. At that point, however, you are on your own. The interview and audition (or screen test) are all dependent on you. If you come through with flying colors and the producer wants you, he calls the agent back. Here again is a critical step. Your agent and the producer bargain for your salary; surprisingly, perhaps, you find you have little to say about it. If all goes well, your agent will get you the best salary the producer is willing to offer; he then calls you and tells you the terms of your employment. In any case you take the job and when you get paid you give your agent whatever percentage of your *gross* income (that income you receive before taxes are deducted) that your agency contract specifies. So the actor-agent relationship is a good one when it works. The actor is spending his time perfecting his craft and the agent is hustling up and down Sunset Boulevard or Seventh Avenue looking for the actor's future job. In theory everything is fine, and frequently everthing *is* fine

Here, however, are the bad things that can happen with an agent.

The agent can ignore you. He can take you on with marvelous promises, take a hundred or so pictures and résumés, and never talk to you again. When this happens you question why he takes you on in the first place. What may have happened is that you have a highly unusual look and the agent is simply going to file your pictures away until he has a call for just that look. Or he took you on as a favor to somebody else who recommended you, or the day after he took you on he found someone just like you but "better," or he only wanted to go to bed with you in the first place and you did not give him a chance. There can be any number of reasons why an agent takes you on and then ignores you. If you have not signed a contract with him, you have not lost anything but the photos. Just ignore *him* and look for somebody else. If you've signed a contract, pester him to death and get him on the stick or get out. Standard agency contracts allow you to terminate your obligations if you have not received 15 days work in the past 91 days.

The agent can promote you for the wrong roles. Agents are not simply clearing offices; they are second-guessers. "I admit, we play God," confesses one. And for good reason. They have been in the business, probably a long time, and they think they know how to market you best. (You may be offended at the terms they use: you are part of their "stable" of talent, you are "marketed" like a cabbage, you are a "juvenile female" instead of an actress.) The agent may have as many as fifty actors under contract, and he cannot send them all out for every role. So the agent may send you only for character roles when you think you can play ingenues, and he may or may not be right.

The agent can be too greedy in your behalf. A friend of ours who sings and plays the guitar was offered a terrific contract at a super-prestigious New York nightclub, where many celebrities got their starts. He had, however, recently signed with an agent who persuaded him he should get more money. He demanded what she said, the offer was withdrawn, and he has never gotten the chance again. Other agents go well beyond persuading you to overreach your salary potential; they demand it in your name without even consulting you. Since the agent bargains directly with the producer before you do, he can keep you out of roles you have successfully auditioned for. No matter that you would work for free in order to get that first credit; your agent may negotiate you right out of it by demanding an extra $25. You may see this as just the chance you take — after all, the agent is interested in the same thing you are, right? Not exactly. The agent is interested in your income, which is not always the same as your total artistic and career growth. The best agents are interested in that, too; the greedy ones want their cut and they want it now. Sympathize with them; they have expensive telephone bills. But be alert. Your best interest and theirs are not always exactly the same.

An agent can give you bad advice. In that, he is no more guilty than anybody else you may come across in your pursuit of success, but it hurts more when your agent does it because you feel obligated to take the advice; in fact you probably *are* obligated to take it if you want the agent to help you. Remember that agents are frequently people who would rather have performed themselves, and part of the pleasure they receive from their work is the vicarious thrill of helping, advising, and nurturing others. Agents, after all, do not live a very glamorous life. They spend most of their time contacting studios, bugging receptionists for scraps of information, and being put on HOLD by the secretaries of those producers and casting directors whose names they are dropping. What they lose in personal self-esteem they sometimes make up by treating you the way they are treated by others. In their offices, *they* know all the answers: how you should act, what your pictures should look like, what acting teacher you should study with, how good you are, how right you are for what role, and how much weight you should lose. Now, in all honesty, we should say that your agent is *probably* right. But the *degree* of probability is not as great as he would have you believe.

We now put the whole thing into perspective with this obvious piece of advice: if you can get an agent, by all means do so. And try and get the very best one for *you* that you can.

Why is that obvious? The agent is on the inside of the business and you are not. From that point of view, every agent is a good agent; some are more careful, likable, honest, and well-known in the business than others, but all franchised agents have access to important contacts that you do not. In New York, despite the open Equity auditions that the union requires, most casting is done through agencies; in Hollywood all of it is. In Hollywood, only a franchised agent can negotiate a contract with a producer: *you* cannot. So if you work in New York, you should do what you can get an agent, or a number of agents, to represent you; and if you work in Hollywood you absolutely *must* have an agent. Only when you become an established star, and can be confident that producers will call you at *your* telephone number, should you consider going it alone.

Getting an agent

How do you go about getting an agent? The first thing you must do is figure out what kind of agent you want. There are hundreds of agents in both major cities, and they can vary enormously in their worth. The difference between having a career and not having one can quite easily depend on which door you knock on first.

The top agents work in their own offices and handle an absolute minimum of clients. One we know handles only six. You need not worry about him; four of those six make among them more than three million dollars a year and the other two make a few thousand each. Why does he handle the other two at all? Because he expects them to be up with the others in a couple of years. Obviously that is the kind of agent you want. Also obviously, that is not the kind of agent you're going to get. Not yet, anyway.

Other agents work in the huge prestige agencies, of which there are three: Creative Management Associates (CMA), International Famous Agency (IFA, formerly Ashley Famous Agency), and the William Morris

Agency. The big agencies have offices in both New York and Los Angeles; each office may have up to fifty agents who handle the affairs of several hundred clients. Not all of these are actors, of course. Some are writers, singers, directors, and musicians, but a large number of them *are* actors, and a lot of those are the people you have heard about since you were twelve. It may do your ego good to be contracted by the same agency that "handles" Peter Fonda and Cary Grant, but remember that a big agency has big clients, that 10 percent of Peter Fonda's income means a lot more to them than 10 percent of your income, that they have a lot of secretaries to pay, and that a young actor can easily get lost in the bureaucratic shuffle.

For a young beginning actor it is probably best to find a small, aggressive agency that is genuinely interested in him. Only then will the actor-agent relationship — a marriage of sorts — prove truly fruitful.

How do you pick a good agent to call on? First of all, the agent *must* be franchised. In Hollywood this means franchised by the Screen Actors' Guild, and in New York by the Actors' Equity Association. Both of these union offices will supply you with a list of franchised agents. Under no circumstances should any actor sign any agreement with a non-franchised agency. Nor, except in highly unusual circumstances, should a young actor sign an agreement with a "personal manager." A personal manager is someone who offers to guide your career in return for a percentage of your income. Since he is not an agent, he cannot negotiate a contract, so you will need an agent as well. He is also not likely to have any special qualifications which would give him the ability to assist your career in any way. In a field already dominated by middlemen, the personal manager seems an unnecessary filter between you, your money, your agent, and your art. The only actors who should take on managers, in our opinion, are (1) those in the $100,000-a-year class, who need business guidance, and (2) those in whose future a potential manager has made a substantial cash investment. This should be done as a strict business proposition, and few managers will suggest it. If *you* do, it will certainly test their seriousness about you.

So you have a list of franchised agents. Still, a list is a list. There are currently 181 agencies (not agents — agencies, with one to fifty agents apiece) franchised by Screen Actors' Guild in Hollywood, and

118 in New York. (Agencies franchised by Equity and AFTRA are virtually the same.) How do you choose the ones to head for first?

Obviously if you have friends in the industry you will ask them for suggestions. Beyond that, here is what you can do, and should do in any case. Look at the published listings of actors and their agents that are available in both cities. In Hollywood this is the *Players' Directory*, which is put out three times a year by the Academy of Motion Picture Arts and Sciences. The *Players' Directory* comes out in two huge volumes that look like giant telephone books; they include two pictures of each actor who pays their fee and the name and address of his agent. You can see the *Players' Directory* in the office of any friendly agent, or you can go to the Academy at 9038 Melrose Avenue, Hollywood 90069, and look at the current edition in the reception room. In New York, the equivalent publication is called the *Players Guide*, and it is available at the publisher's office, 165 West 46th Street.

These books are valuable for you to examine merely in order to gauge the competition. You will probably find a depressing number of faces that look pretty good. Look in the pages that list actors of your character type. Find an agency that seems to have a few unknowns in your field. They are good places to start, and if they are over-full in your type, they may recommend you to some agency that is not. By studying these guides, you can get some sort of picture of which agents are handling which kinds of clients, and you will get an idea as to where to start.

From these sources you should be able to find the names of ten to fifteen smallish agencies that handle people like yourself and are probably interested in taking on new clients. Perhaps you can rank them in order of desirability, particularly if any of them have been especially recommended by someone you trust. Now you must call on them.

Agents are busy people and they are not going to be eager to see you if you just pop in and announce yourself. In fact, many agents are loath to see *any* inexperienced actor-hopefuls. Unless you do things the right way, you will not get past the receptionist. Here are the time-honored ways of making that first appointment — in order of their effectiveness.

By far the easiest way is through a personal contact. There is the dirty word again, and it is as important as ever. Frankly, most agents will not bother to see *anybody* without a personal reference from someone in the business whom they know. Your best chance of getting an agent, if you can swing it, is to be recommended by a working producer. If a producer is behind you, the agent will feel that you already have a leg up on getting work; besides, by taking you on, the agent may be able to broaden *his* own contacts at the same time. Remember, like you, the agent is always looking to strengthen his contacts. But even if the contact is just another actor who recommends that you see his agent (which, ordinarily, only an actor of the opposite sex is likely to do), the contact is a valuable way to get your foot in the door.

If you lack a personal contact, your next best means of landing an agent is to be *seen* in something. This involves getting a fairly good role in a showcase or workshop production. In New York these are called off-off-Broadway productions; in Los Angeles they are just called workshops. Via agreements with the acting union, workshop productions can be presented for nominal admission fees and for limited runs even though professional actors are used. Getting a good part in one is not by any means automatic, but you can quickly find your way around to their auditions. In New York, the trade papers and *The Village Voice* are good sources of information about the off-off-Broadway market; in Los Angeles the trade papers and the *Los Angeles Free Press* will let you know what is going on. Union offices in both cities are also good sources of casting information for workshop productions.

If you are in a workshop, you will probably be seen by agents even if you do not do another thing. Part of the agent's job consists of scouting new talent, and these workshop productions are among his chief sources. Productions at the good local colleges (UCLA and USC in Los Angeles; Yale and NYU in New York) are frequently visited by New York agents. But by all means, this is the time for you to contact agents and invite them to come. You will invariably do this first by letter (which you should personally deliver) — a letter which includes your photo-résumé and an invitation to see the production at the agent's convenience. You should leave this letter off about two weeks before the production opens and then follow up with a telephone call a few days before opening night.

"Hi," you say in your most unaffected voice, "I'm Tondolaya Schwartzkov, and I left a photo and résumé at your office a couple of weeks ago? . . . Yes . . . and I'd like to see if you would be able to come to see me in *Bloodbath* at the Actors' Experimental Lab any time next week? Friday? I'll leave off the tickets today."

And you do. Hopefully you get several to come on different nights. If they come on the same night, don't worry about it. Let them compete for you. If you are any good they will be backstage afterwards to talk shop with you.

You need not be in a production for an agent to see you act. A third way of making the agent aware of you is simply to send the agent a letter and a photo-résumé and then call and ask for an appointment. Even with no contacts and no chance to see you in performance, an agent could become interested. If you send out a dozen or two letters, you should get one or two bites. When you call for an appointment the agent will probably ask you to perform a scene in his office, and if he likes it, and you, a working relationship may be forthcoming.

Interviewing an agent

Once you have finally contacted an agent, he will ask you to his office for an interview, at which he will determine whether or not to take you on. Since you will be interviewing for most of the roles you will get, you must treat the interview with the agent just as seriously as an interview with a producer or director. The agent will be trying to see if you interview as well as you act, and it is important that you impress upon him that you do.

If you are invited to "come in and talk," set up an appointment and keep it exactly. Come on time, and come in looking your best. If you look your best in jeans and a Mickey Mouse tee shirt, wear them, but be clean, neat, and striking. "Look like an actor and act like an actor," cautions one agent. Be at ease and be yourself. Agents are not always very good at interviewing people; they are apt to be unsure of what to ask and generally nervous. Help the agent interview you. Tell him about your career, your desires, your commitment, your training, what you feel you can do, and what sacrifices you are prepared to make. Answer his questions truthfully. An agent is like a lawyer: you have to trust him completely. If there is any lying to be done about your career, you will want him to do it, not you. Impress on the agent that you want to become a working professional actor, and

Acting Professionally

that you have a realistic outlook about your future. Do not presume to know more than he does about show business, even if you think you do. Terminate the interview when you think you have said and asked everything on your mind. Some people do not know when to quit talking, and some agents do not know how to get people out of their offices. Offer to leave when you sense the interview is over, and go home or see a movie.

The agent will rarely offer you a contract on the spot. He may want to think you over, to consult with colleagues, and to check his files for available jobs in your category. If he wants you, he will let you know, either by grabbing you before you leave the office or by calling you later. Your task is simply to keep trying until someone grabs you.

Occasionally the agent will ask you to do a scene in his office, particularly if he has never seen you act. In this case, be prepared to do so. You will be doing so often in your career, and this is a good time to get started. See the section on prepared scenes; those principles apply here.

Eventually an agent will decide to take you on as a client. In Hollywood you will sign an exclusive contract for the agent to represent you in all dramatic camera media. This is a regulation of the Screen Actors' Guild; only a franchised agent can negotiate a contract, and an actor may be represented by only one franchised agent. You can, if you so desire, have another agent for commercials, and another for live theatre, but frequently in Hollywood you will simply have one agent who will handle you in all media. In New York the practice is somewhat different. There agents may take you on without signing you to exclusive contracts. An actor in New York may have working agreements (written or otherwise) with any number of agents at the same time. In New York, where an actor can get along fairly well without an agent at all, the agent's position is more that of a booking agent; he has a roster of jobs that he tries to apportion among a roster of clients before another agent gets to them. New York agents hustle a lot, as a result, but it is also easy to get lost in the shuffle of their rosters. It is desirable, therefore, to establish a solid, trusting relationship with a New York agent as well: one who is deeply committed to you and your success.

If you sign with an agent, or have an agent working for you, you have entered into a partnership which it is hoped will prove beneficial to both of you. At this point you have by no means "made it"; you are still just beginning. If your agent is a good one, he will take a profound interest in your career. He will advise you as to photographs, he will make up your new résumé, and he will try to introduce you to the right people at the right time. He will get your pictures into the *Players' Directory* or *Players' Guide* (though you pay the fee). He will manage your career. It is vital that you establish a trusting relationship. This takes patience on your part. Frequently an actor signs with an agent, and then, three months later, having had no significant results, he starts shopping for another. The business does not work that way. Your agent will need time to get to know you and your work; he will try to establish your image together with his own in the memory of the producers with whom he comes in contact. One agent estimates that it takes about a year for the agent to really establish his client in the overall market picture, and another two years to get offers coming in with any regularity — and that is if things go well. The third year, he says, is usually when the payoff comes, if it does. The actor who impatiently switches agents over and over again merely starts anew each time and never has the chance to establish an image in the industry.

Each agent, however, has his own point of view, and an agent whose plan to market you is a bad one is ultimately of little use to you. You want an agent who, whatever his standing, is enthusiastic about you and sees you pretty much the way you want to be seen. If you want to play classical tragedy and he wants to sell you for *Hee Haw*, you had better get things straight before you sign. No agent will be offended if you simply ask: "How do you see me?" Let him tell you; you may be astonished at what he sees. Give him the benefit of the doubt, if there is one. You might be a lot better in *Hee Haw* than in *Hamlet*. On the other hand, you may not want to spend the rest of your life with *Hee Haw* and its ilk, so you have some decisions to make.

If you are lucky enough to find an agent who sees you the way you wish to be seen, take him and do what he says. Accept his judgment on your photographs, what you should wear, how you should do your hair, how much weight you should lose, and so forth. Talk things over, but be prepared to trust him. Nobody's advice is perfect, but your agent is your partner, and the two of you had better be working together and not at odds with each other.

Rounds

What does the actor do all day when he is not working? He goes on his rounds. This is as time-honored as the opening night party at Sardi's. With a good pair of shoes, or a good clutch in the Volkswagen, the actor goes to see everybody and anybody who can get him a job in the theatre.

Rounds in New York are much more part of an actor's daily routine than they are in Hollywood, and an actor there can go out on rounds without an agent or a union card to pave the way. The goal of making rounds is to see as many producers and agents as possible and make them aware of your presence and your availability. You should first check the regular casting notices posted on the Equity office bulletin board (165 West 46th Street) and in the casting pages of *Variety, Backstage,* and *Show Business,* and then visit the producers' offices with copies of your photo-résumé to leave off. You can follow up these visits with a call or repeat visit to see if any action has been taken yet. You will rarely get further than the receptionist's office, but do not despair. Making rounds is an ego-busting trip anyway, and you must not let it get to you. The receptionist generally will transmit whatever material you give her, and if there is a chance for you, you will hear about it.

After going to the producers who you know are casting, you then head for those about whom you know nothing. You can simply look up the names of active producers and agents in the yellow pages of the Manhattan Telephone Directory and follow them up. Or better, you can take a walk over to the Drama Book Shop (150 West 52nd Street) and purchase a current geographical guide to New York casting offices. There are two of these published regularly, under somewhat different names (see Appendix). Both are mimeographed lists of agents' and producers' offices arranged by street as well as alphabetically. Thus, in a selected itinerary, you could visit the thirty-odd offices on 57th Street in an afternoon without ever retracing your steps. These little books (they cost under $2.00, and either one will do) are worth a mint in saving you time and shoe leather. The Drama Book Shop is also a worthwhile regular stop on your daily rounds; the bulletin board sporadically lists casting opportunities, and the shop, which sells virtually every theatre publication available in English, offers a superb collection of fact sheets, pamphlets, and books which are helpful to theatre people like yourself.

In Hollywood, your rounds are mainly restricted to producers of commercials; the producers of television and film shows are accessible only by an appointment arranged by your agent. (Many New York producers are available solely in that fashion also.) But the commercial producers are many, and many can be visited without an appointment. Get a list from your agent or from *Simon's Directory of Theatrical Materials, Services and Information* and map yourself out an itinerary. It is desirable to call commercial agencies first and ask for an appointment; you can still manage to see several in a day's time if you avoid rush hours and long cross-town trips. One discouraging note, maybe: a Screen Actors' Guild union card (see Unions, page 80) is almost essential to land commercial work, unless you have some highly specialized ability or characteristic that they need. With your SAG card, however, and a good photo-résumé, you might get somewhere in the commercial field, which can not only make you a lot of money (residual payments frequently go into the thousands and tens of thousands for long running commercials) but also will allow you to be seen by thousands of producers when they watch Johnny Carson after work. Not a few actors have gotten their first real break after being seen in a bright, novel "commersh."

Interviews

Interviews are as much a make-or-break step on the road to getting a role as any other single factor. The interview takes place when the producer has called *you* (as contrasted to your rounds, where you are calling on him). Thus, with an interview, you at least know you are in contention for something, even though hundreds of others may share your status. In Hollywood, particularly, the majority of roles are cast solely on the basis of interviews; in fact, working professional film actors make it a point of personal privilege never to audition; they simply meet the producer, who either is already familiar with their work or can call up film on the actors from the vaults. But if you have not worked, or you are in New York, the interview is merely a milepost on the road to an audition. And you must pass the milepost with elan.

Interviews are a great stumbling block for many actors. "I don't interview well" is a common complaint, and actors who have been trained to play characters with strength, compassion, and subtlety fall completely to pieces when they are asked to play themselves. For that is what you do in an interview: you play yourself. You must not pretend for a moment that an interview is simply a casual, obligatory preface to an audition. The interview is a stage on which million-dollar decisions are made, and despite the general and desirable state of informality, you are being examined very closely — and you must perform.

The interview is calculated to let the producer know just what kind of person you are. As we discussed earlier, film and television directors rely heavily on your personality rather than your acting ability. "Casting people are afraid of people who *act*," is an often-voiced Hollywood complaint, and doubtless this is in many cases true. Because of the extremely limited rehearsal time for most television shows (and many films and plays, for that matter), producers are always partial to the actor whose own personality closely matches the characterization they want. Remember too, they have literally thousands of people to choose from; why should they take someone 6'3" when they want, and can easily get, someone who's 6'2"? Casting decisions are rarely that specific as to height, but if you translate that into subjective qualities, you begin to see how little compromise they have to make.

How do you perform in an interview? You play yourself, to be sure, and you must do it honestly. That involves a slight contradiction in terms, to be sure, but remember: all behavior, as well as all acting, is a combination of honest self-expression and transmission of an image. You are entitled to select which aspects of yourself you want to display. Be yourself, but be your *best* self. You are an actor: look like it and act like it. You are a professional: let them know it. Arrive on time, prepared with your photo-résumé and a book of pictures of yourself. Relax and let your salable qualities shine. Ask questions. Be vivacious, not retiring. Be friendly but not self-effacing. Be funny, if you feel like it, but not at your own (or their) expense. In short, sell yourself without blasting them out of the room.

What will you face? Usually one producer — maybe two or three; maybe a casting director or two; and maybe a secretary or another actor who happens to be in the room with you. You will be introduced to everyone; try to remember their names (and, when you leave the office, write them down for future reference). Your first look when you walk in the door tells them 75 percent of what they wanted to know already. Make it a good look. Be confident, be attractive, and show those things which you consider your personal assets. Then sit down and get them to talk to you.

Without fail you will be asked, "Well, tell me about yourself." There it is: the one big identity question that has shrivelled some actors into their own neuroses so far that they can only stammer their name, rank, and social security number. Be prepared for it. There are no rules for interviews, no forms to fill out. If you begin by telling them all your problems, the interview is over before it begins. "Well, I suppose you want to know about my credits. I don't have any." Only a psychologist can explain why so many actors destroy themselves daily by such remarks. Tell them about yourself honestly but positively: "I want to become a working professional actor . . . I've studied with this teacher and that one. . . . I played *Coriolanus* at Ashland. . . . I'm a short story writer with *Argosy* magazine." Tell them things you would like them to know and avoid things you would rather they did not know. Nobody has asked you to present both sides of the case, and believe us, they have every reason in the world *not* to cast you, so don't make that decision any easier for them.

Producers see a great many people when they are casting, so it certainly does not hurt to be memorable. If you can look memorable, or say something memorable, or do something memorable, it helps. Mere politeness (which, after all, you must practice) is not enough to stimulate anybody's interest; everybody is polite. While it is hardly recommended, a downright hostile attitude at the end of a wearying day has sometimes aroused a little excitement in a casting director, although it rarely has produced an actual offer. Find an exciting way to be different.

Interviewing takes some practice. No amount of advice is helpful after the first few interviews, because everyone must find his own style of "being himself" and being himself memorably. You should go to every interview you possibly can, because with each you will acquire not only valuable know-how, but a confidence which is necessary and which you can never fake. It takes most people ten or fifteen interviews before they finally start to "come out," since the tendency of most sensitive people (and most actors are sensitive people) is to sit docilely in an overstuffed chair and answer the questions they are asked as simply as possible. If you breathe a sigh of relief when an interview is over, you probably have not done a very good job. Conversely, if you feel you have met some interesting people, then they probably feel the same way about you, and you probably have done well.

A final suggestion: get to know the secretaries and receptionists. You need all the friends you can find.

Auditions

Auditions are the means by which the stage actor and the beginning film actor show the producers what they can do. If you are at the beginning of your career, it is absolutely essential that you learn to audition and to audition well. Again, actors have all sorts of hang-ups about auditions, and many feel they audition poorly but act magnificently. If that is your hang-up, you will simply have to get over it. Producers with thousands of actors to choose from do not need to bother having faith in you. They will choose someone who they *know* can do the role, and they know it on the basis of his superior audition.

There are two types and two locations for auditions. The types are the prepared scene and the cold reading. The locations are the producer's office and the stage. You must be prepared for all four combinations.

Prepared scenes are the actor's opportunity to show himself at his best. You should have two or three scenes in varying styles ready to go on a day's notice. For stage work your audition scenes should preferably be monologues; for film and television auditions you should prepare scenes with a partner. Choose your scenes and rehearse them carefully. In choosing scenes for prepared auditions, keep in mind:

A prepared scene should be short. Five minutes is the absolute maximum, and three is usually desirable. Your scene should be long enough to produce impact, and then end. Though few actors are aware of it, the producer generally gets all the information he wants in the first few seconds of your audition; the rest of the time he is quite possibly thinking of something (or someone) else.

The prepared scene should show you in a role in which you could be cast *today*. Particularly if you are auditioning for a film or television role, do something very close to your age and personality, and something in a style as close as possible to the style of the part for which you are auditioning. If you are auditioning at Screen Gems, it is silly to do a scene from *Othello*. Even if you played old ladies in college, you will not do them on Broadway, so don't give them your Aunt Eller until you are in your fifties.

Choose audition material that is self-explanatory. In no case should you explain, before your audition, the plot of the scene or the characterization you are trying to convey. At most you should say the name of the scene and proceed.

Choose audition material that is not shopworn. Every year there are a few "in" audition pieces which generally mean instant death for the poor actor doing them before a group that has seen them fifty times. It is fun and frequently rewarding to find scenes in contemporary novels and extract them for audition material; chances are the dialogue is realistic and the auditioners will be interested in seeing something new. Remember, they are judging you, not the material, and it does not have to be a masterpiece for them to like you doing it.

Choose scenes that can be done without extensive movement or many properties. You may have to do them in a producer's office with only a few square feet to move around in and with your "audience" only a few inches away. Practice your scenes this way so that the conditions will not throw you. Also practice them in a variety of locations so that you can adjust movement at will and without advance preparation.

Keep your scenes loose, and not dependent on any single planned "effect." Let the environment of your performance, whether it be office or stage, affect what you and your partner do. Some actors prefer just to run lines with their partner and not rehearse at all, in order to achieve greater freedom and spontaneity during the actual audition. If this works for you, do it; remember that the producer is not looking for a complete performance, but for your ability to act convincingly (and, when you have a partner, to *react* convincingly, as well).

Choose your acting partner carefully. You must trust him completely. He should be willing to give you focus if it is your audition. You might respond by working up some scenes in which he has focus for his auditions. But no matter whose scene it is, you look better if he is good than if he is bad, so do not grab a bad partner in the hopes that he will make you look good.

If you are permitted, or required, to do two scenes, choose two that differ in tone and style rather than in age. Generally you are asked to do contrasting scenes, such as comedy and drama, or (particularly with stage work) classical and modern. Do not think of these categories as absolute, and do not worry too much about whether *Tartuffe* is funny or serious or whether *St. Joan* is modern or classical. The point is to get two differing scenes that show you off to your best advantage. If you are confused about what kinds of scenes they want, ask.

Above all, choose material that shows you at your best. Ultimately, that is your overriding concern. You do not want your audition scenes to be merely good; you want them to be terrific. Choose material at which you excel, even if it means not doing exactly what they have asked or we have suggested. The audition fails if you do not come off looking better than anybody they have seen that day, and a merely competent job with material you do not like is as bad as nothing at all. Have your agent preview your audition pieces and comment. If you are doing a full stage audition, such as the Chicago auditions, by all means get a director to help you and work on your audition until you are satisfied that it shows off your best qualities.

Auditions and interviews are both competitions, and you must treat them as such. You are being examined for your usefulness in an industry that wants to make money by your efforts. There are many competitors for every job; they are, in effect, put on a treadmill and passed in front of the casting directors and producers. It is your task to stop the treadmill and make the auditioners take notice of your individual value to their enterprise. Whatever you can do (within the bounds of your own personality and ethics) to accomplish that, you ought to do.

Prepared scenes are generally requested when the actor has not been seen. TCG, regional repertory companies, and most New York theatre producers will see prepared scenes at regular intervals, ordinarily at the request of an actor or his agent. Agents frequently ask to see prepared scenes from actors they are interested in representing. Most Hollywood casting offices set aside one or two days a month to see prepared audition scenes from new talent referred to them by agents. Except in the case of those regional repertory auditions, where actors are hired for an entire season at a time, prepared scene auditions rarely lead directly to employment. Most often they serve simply to introduce the actor to producers who might some day want to use him. Most audition scenes are viewed without respect to specific casting availabilities.

Cold readings are the next step towards a job. In a cold reading you are called in, given a copy of a script, and asked to read it and act it for the producers. In a cold reading, you are going for a specific part, and at least you know that a part exists. If you are right for it, you may get it. You read, either alone or with the stage manager, the producer, or another actor auditioning for another role, and you stop when you are told. Your reading may be on a stage or in an office. Your object, quite obviously, is to be overwhelmingly good.

A cold reading need not be entirely cold, and if the idea of cold readings frightens you (and it should) there is plenty you can do about it. Ordinarily you can read the script beforehand — perhaps in the office waiting room. Sometimes you can get the script the day before. Generally they will at least offer you the chance to skim the text, and naturally you should take it. If not, you can always ask a couple of questions. Frequently actors feel they should not ask the director what he wants. Directors, however, are paid to answer actors' questions. Certainly you should make sure of the character's basic intentions, age, and characteristics if they are not evident in what you see. Try and put that all into one question, and then let the director talk as long as he wishes.

Do not worry if you cannot pronounce certain words or if you muff lines. Nobody expects a finished performance at a cold reading, and no good directors care at this point for perfection of detail. What they are looking for is that germ of characterization they find essential to the part. If you have it, and they are confident you can get the rest in the time available, you will be in the running. If, however, you get flustered merely because you cannot pronounce the character's name, your lack of confidence may ruin your performance.

It is best to avoid heavy characterization in a cold reading, unless you are *certain* that is what is required. If you are not, be as natural as possible; read the character as if he were you, or you were he, and let the director see your basic personal quality in your acting. If the role requires an accent and you can do it, do it; if you can't, don't. In general do not try anything that may make you look bad unless they ask you to do so.

Most cold readings are terminated by the director when he has found out what he wants to know. Sometimes, however, he seems uncertain. He doesn't ask you to leave, but you can tell that he is not entirely satisfied, either. He is making up his mind. This is a good time to ask him, for example, "Do you think in this scene Martha would be a little more compassionate?" You might get a little direction and a chance to do it again in a manner closer to the director's idea of the part. Remember, the director cannot read your mind and he probably assumes that if you did not read the role with more compassion, it was because you could not. Both directors and actors have an odd way of assuming that their interpretations are universally understood. Always look for any information you can get on what the director or producer wants, and use it. If he coaches you, listen. Unless you are quite certain of your indispensability, this is not the time to debate his points.

If you sing, you may be invited to audition for musical plays or films. You should be prepared to sing a song or two for the producers, and if you can get the music to one of the songs in the production being done, do so. You should bring your own music to a musical audition, properly marked for the transpositions and tempos that you wish to use. You may wish to hire your own accompanist to rehearse with you and accompany you. This is standard practice in all professional auditions, since poor accompaniment (even from a good musician who simply has not rehearsed with you) can ruin your presentation.

Sometimes in an audition or an interview you will be asked to take off your clothes. Contemporary films frequently involve nudity, and so, increasingly, does contemporary theatre. There are strict union regulations regarding this, and you should be aware of them. It is entirely proper for a director to get some idea of what your body looks like, and he might ask you to show him without having you undress. Under no circumstances, however, may he ask you to undress without having informed you when the appointment was made that the part involves nudity and that you will be asked to disrobe during audition. This at least gives you time to check out the producer and make sure you know what you are getting into. Remember that your agent and the union (even if you are not a member) will protect you from unscrupulous voyeurs who happen to be producing films and plays. On the other hand, if you plan to do nude films or plays, you had better plan on doing nude auditions as well.

You will have to adopt a pretty stable audition attitude. Like everything else in the life of a beginning professional actor, auditions can lead to paranoia. Even if everybody from the producer on down is extremely polite, you are nevertheless unceremoniously directed to perform when they ask you and to leave when they tell you. Frequently you are ushered onto a stage and see nothing in front of you but bright lights and a few shadowy forms at the back, and you hear nothing but "Name!" "Well, let's see it!" and, in the middle of your prepared monologue, "Thank you very much. Next please!" It is discouraging to the strong and ruinous to the weak, and you had better be prepared for it. A professional attitude is your point of strength. Remember always that you have to stop the treadmill. Only if you are solidly confident can you be strong enough to do that.

The screen test

Screen tests are used in Hollywood to see how you look on camera. The screen test may be a very simple affair whereby you turn your face from left to right in front of a camera and speak some lines or improvise a conversation. Or it can be as involved as a complete scene that you rehearse with a studio director and perform with sets and costumes. For major roles in films and television series, the screen test is usually the last stage of the audition, and the finalists for a certain role may screen-test opposite each other. Only newcomers are screen-tested, however, since veteran actors can be seen by studio executives in actual film or taped performances available to them on call.

Screen tests are not universally used any more, and many producers have no time for them at all. Paul Monash cast Michael Sacks, a twenty-two-year-old actor with no professional acting experience whatever, as the lead in *Slaughterhouse Five* without a test, declaring he did not believe in them. Nevertheless, be prepared to do a screen test, since you might well be asked for one. Naturally the more experience you have had before a camera, the better, so seize every opportunity to perform and see yourself in student films and even home movies.

The job offer

If you have played all your cards right, if you are as good as you think you are, and if your contacts, interviews, auditions, and readings have gone well, you may be offered a part. You now have to decide whether you will take it or not. For most actors, this is the easiest decision of their lives.

There are some jobs, however, that you might want to think twice about taking, even if they are the first thing that comes your way.

The job could be a non-union job. Many theatres and independent film companies skirt union regulations and jurisdiction. Even though they may pay you a union scale wage, they do not operate according to certain procedures which the union requires of all producers. Check with the union. If the producer is operating in frank violation of union regulations, you may find yourself blackballed from future employment. This is rare, but investigate. If it happens to you, you may never live it down.

The job could be quasi-union. That is, it could be a workshop or experimental production (student films come under this category) that operates under a special dispensation from the union. In which case you are liable not to be paid, or to be given "deferred payment," which means you will not get the money until the project is successfully marketed. If the project is non-union but operated in accordance with the union, you have nothing to fear from participating, but you might not get more out of it than the work itself.

The job could be union but distant. For example, you could be hired for two months in June to work bit parts at an Equity dinner theatre in Williamsburg, Virginia. So while you are carrying spears and inviting the guests to dinner in Virginia (for a salary that doesn't permit you to keep your New York digs) you're missing important Broadway and off-Broadway auditions in the city.

The job could be a nudie film or play. These come in two categories. The independent non-union X-rated films (and stage equivalents) are utterly useless to you except as a source of income, and the income is pretty low. The days are over when an actress had her career ruined because she posed in the nude, but we have not reached the point when her career would be particularly helped by being featured in one of the cunnilingus and fellatio flicks. Even the major studio pornographic films offer little besides more money and a chance to roll around with some attractive strangers in the nude.

Then there are "serious" nude films, or rather, serious films that have nude sequences. Every young actor today, particularly in films, should expect to be asked, sometime early in his career, to do a nude scene. The answer that most will give — that they will do it as long as it is tastefully done — is not really to the point, since the producer will invariably tell you that it will be tastefully done, and until the final cut you have no idea exactly what that means; and, possibly, neither does he. At any rate, do not for a moment think that "if they want me badly enough, they'll get a double for the nude scenes." They will not want you that badly.

Doing nude scenes in films may be even harder than you think. If it were a matter of simply flipping off a robe, shooting a quick scene, and then dressing again, that would be one thing. More often, even for a simple ten-second shot, many hours of takes and retakes will be required. You might find yourself standing, sitting, and lying around in the nude amidst fifty technicians, actors, and producers (all fully dressed) while they take, focus, retake, and refocus your ten-second nude scene. Strong, uninhibited actresses have been reduced to quivering tears by this dehumanizing process, which, after all, is exactly the device the Nazis used to humiliate and interrogate political prisoners.

The role may be otherwise offensive. It may be pornographic, or simply too small, or the style of the material may be too clichéd and ridiculous for your taste and talent. You may be asked to work with actors or directors you do not respect, or in a television show you loathe. You may be asked to do a commercial for a product you find personally disgusting, or to do an accent you find ethnically or racially degrading.

There are, then, a number of reasons why you may *not* accept every job that comes your way. As usual, there are two schools of thought about this. Lucille Ball once said that the way she got to the top of her profession was by taking absolutely every job she could get. Others have preferred to wait until the "right one" comes up. Obviously every time you accept a job you thereby deny yourself the opportunity to take others at the same time and you miss auditions that you would otherwise be free to attend. But then every decision you will make in your career necessitates choosing one route and abandoning others; in the end a lot depends on luck in making the right choices. Perhaps that job in Williamsburg will lead to another one in New Haven, which will lead to a Broadway role. An actor of our acquaintance who performed regularly for ten years admits that every single job he had (except the first) came from a previous job. So Lucy Ball's advice is sound; and a beginning actor should refuse a union job only for extraordinarily compelling reasons.

Unions

If you accept a union job, you will now join the appropriate union. The three dramatic unions, which have been mentioned frequently herein, are the Screen Actors' Guild (SAG), which handles all filmed acting (including filmed television shows and filmed commercials); Actors' Equity Association, which handles all live theatre performing, and the American Federation of Television and Radio Artists (AFTRA) which handles all live and videotaped television programming and commercials, as well as radio broadcasting. These unions are joined together with a few others in a loose association referred to as the Associated Actors and Artists of America (the Four A's), which also includes the American Guild of Variety Artists (AGVA), the American Guild of Musical Artists (AGMA), and the Screen Extras' Guild (SEG). The unions seem a huge barrier to the non-member beginner. And they are meant to do so. The business of unions is to protect the membership's ability to land paying jobs, and to keep producers from hiring non-union persons at less than union minimum wages.

You cannot join the unions without a union job, and you cannot get a union job without belonging to the union. This is the big nut you have to crack, and it's a tough one. But there are 15,000 members in Equity and 24,000 members in SAG, so obviously it can be done.

To get a fair perspective, you must look at the industry from the union's point of view as well as your own. From the outside, your exclusion from many casting opportunities seems unfair; particularly when you find that a producer must pay a fine of $100, in certain jurisdictions and under certain conditions, in order to sign a non-union performer to a union contract. But if you aspire to become a working professional, then you will eventually crack the union and their regulations will protect *you*. After all, there are thousands of actors coming out of colleges every year who would be only too happy to perform small film roles for $5.00 a day. How can working professionals protect themselves against that? If the union regulations were somehow lifted, chaos would result, and hardly any actor could make a living.

Remember, the union would only get richer (at first) if it accepted initiation fees from everybody who wanted to join. That they do not do this is a testimony that they wish to maintain the integrity of the union as an association of working professionals.

Joining one of the AAAA unions should be a first priority item on your agenda. Only with union membership does the full range of casting and audition opportunities begin to open up to you; most auditions in both New York and Hollywood are posted for Equity actors (or SAG actors) only. Obviously you are going to have to break into one of the off-Broadway, regional theatre, or summer stock shows that will hear non-union auditionees, or one of the television programs or films that screen-tests unknowns. Once you join the union, you can automatically join the others by payment of a fee, which is about half the original initiation fee. Full initiation fees are currently $200 (Equity) and $250 (SAG).

When you join the union, you can take advantage of union benefits. Each has a regular magazine for members, keeping them up to date on union activities and services. Union offices can offer help and advice, and will act upon complaints about unscrupulous producers or agents. It is important that, during the time you are working toward a position as a professional actor, you keep up your union dues payments and keep in good standing. It is also important that you obey union rules and do not try to act in unauthorized productions which are expressly forbidden by your union.

Your union will provide you with current information as to minimum salary scales and working conditions; you should be aware of them and make sure they apply to you. You will be amazed at the number of ways you can be hired and paid according to union-negotiated contracts. The Screen Actors' Guild has negotiated contracts with film producers and television producers which run into hundreds of pages and cover every possible variation of employment. Actors' Equity Association has not only contracted with the League of New York Theatres (the basic contract) and with LORT, but also with the Council of Stock Theatres (COST), the Council of Resident Stock Theatres (CORST), and the Association of Civic Musical Theatres (ACMT), and handles, in addition, an off Broadway contract, a Hollywood theatre contract, an off-Loop contract for Chicago, a Bay Area contract for San Francisco, a Las Vegas contract, a contract for the producers of industrial shows, a cafe contract, a guest artist contract, and a dinner theatre contract. These all differ markedly in their provisions, and you will find that there are hundreds of pay scales for various union dramatic activities.

Ordinarily you will join the union automatically with your first professional job. Ideally, your first salary will cover your initiation cost. If it does not, you will have to have the money available somewhere. A provision of the Taft-Hartley Law will permit you to pay after you have been paid, so that will take some of the sting out of it. In addition, AFTRA rules allow you to do one role, and as many more as you can squeeze into the following thirty days, without joining the union. But thirty-one days later, your next AFTRA role will require you to join.

How much will you make?

You have a job. Now that you have struggled, humbled yourself, and suffered financial hardships by the carload, you are ready to cash in your chips, right? What will the job pay?

As we've frequently averred, the median annual income for *working* professional actors is around $1100. (In 1967, for which complete figures are available, 8,500 SAG members earned less than $1000, and 10,900 earned more. Of that 10,900, nearly two-thirds earned less than $5000.) But if you get work, you do get paid for it, and you should know just how much you can expect.

All the unions have negotiated contracts in your behalf; these contracts specify the minimum salaries you will be paid. The minimum salary scales are written in astonishing detail; the Codified Basic Agreement negotiated between the Screen Actors' Guild and the various motion picture producers is a 172-page book. The contracts are renegotiated continuously upon expiration, so the following information, which is accurate as of this printing, is subject to regular change.

If you land a part in a Broadway play, your minimum salary will be $185 a week in 1971-2, $197.50 a week in 1972-3, and $210 a week in 1973-4.

If you land a part in an off-Broadway play, your salary will be at least $100 to $175 a week, depending on the gross receipts of the theatre, in 1970-71. These figures will increase $12.50 per week annually through the duration of the present contract (until 1974).

If you are cast as a member of a regional repertory company, you will be paid a minimum ranging from $112.50 per week to $174.90 per week, depending on the maximum potential weekly gross receipts of the theatre. ($24,000 gives the theatre an "A" rating with Equity, and gives you the maximum scale pay.)

If you are cast in a stock company, you will receive a minimum of $138.20 per week.

If you find employment acting in films or television shows, you are paid either by the day or by the week. Established scale wages for SAG performers are $138 per day or $483 per week, although there are other forms of contract (such as term contracts) which cover longer stretches of time and involve less pay per week.

If you perform under an AFTRA contract and have a part with more than five lines, you can expect to receive at least $110 for one day's work on a 15-minute show, or $350 for five days work on a two-hour show.

But these are just scale figures. Obviously you can negotiate (or your agent can negotiate) for more. What are your negotiating tools? They are not the same as those qualities which got you the job in the first place. Your salary will be determined mainly by your *name* and by the producer's need to have you. An industry is an industry, and nobody is going to spend $1000 for you when he can get someone just as good for $138.

Beginners start out at scale, although a featured performer in a television show (more than a couple of lines) will probably get a little more: maybe $150 a day instead of $138.

Established performers whose names are known to the industry, if not to the public at large, may get, for a television show, $250 to $350 a day, or perhaps three days work for $750, or a week's work for $1000. Stage actors work for close to minimum figures off-Broadway, and journeyman actors usually receive from $200 to $400 for stage work on the LORT circuit and for non-starring Broadway roles. While these figures are obviously "rule of thumb," you should realize that a free-lance actor *with a good reputation in the trade* can work fairly regularly and still not make more than $10,000 a year in direct salary payments on television (ten guest spots), films (five weeks' work on each of two films), or live theatre (a thirty-week run at $325). That's a living wage, to be sure, but you will have to be very lucky and very good to get it. And next year, of course, you might have half that.

Bigger money comes to the performer who lands a regular run in a television series; this occasionally happens to relatively inexperienced new performers. Even though an unknown performer can start out on a series making as little (relatively) as $400 per week, the regularity of the work multiplies this into a handsome sum. A person contracted to a series is guaranteed at least seven segments and generally will work at least thirteen. Regular salaries of up to $1000 per segment can be paid to virtual newcomers if they are cast as leading series performers, and this mounts steadily as the series goes on year after year. The stars of *Bonanza* earned $16,000 each per episode in 1971 and negotiated a contract which raises their salary $1000 per segment in succeeding years. In recent years, however, the number of segments made annually has dropped from thirty-nine to about fifteen or seventeen for most shows. Established Broadway performers make from $250 to $1000 a week, depending on the size of the part and the size of the budget; the Broadway actor's security comes from the length of an extended run.

With name stars, every rule of thumb goes out the window. A name star is someone whose name alone will bring people to the box office (or bring the Nielsen families to their television sets). Stars, of course, get what the traffic will bear, and it was not too long ago that salaries of $1,000,000 per film were paid to the likes of Paul Newman, Elizabeth Taylor, and Marlon Brando. Those days are not definitely over, but big stars now often perform for expenses, and take a percentage of the production's gross receipts or profits instead. To get a star, a TV producer whose top salary offer is ordinarily $1500 may offer $2500; a Broadway producer may offer $5000 per week or more, while the rest of the cast is working for scale.

Residuals are an important source of income for the television actor. The salary you are paid for acting in a television production covers the first showing only. During the summer rerun of an SAG-authorized production, the actor receives another salary equal to 50 percent of his original paycheck. If the production is run a third time, he receives another 40 percent of his original paycheck. If it is syndicated and runs forever, like some segments of *I Love Lucy*, he receives 25 percent each time for runs four, five, and six, and 15 percent for seven, eight, nine, and ten. AFTRA has a similar arrangement. Although most shows are not broadcast more than three times, the actor can expect to receive, after a couple of years, a sum roughly equal to his original check. If it runs forever, he stands to collect a bundle. Agents take commissions only on the first two reruns.

Residuals become vital to the income of actors appearing in television commercials, of course. For a filmed television commercial, the beginning actor will invariably be paid a scale wage of $136. However, he is paid residuals whenever the commercial is aired. It is not true that he will be paid each and every time it is shown; the contract gives him, via an incredibly complex computation, up to $700+ for each thirteen-week period in which the commercial is seen. Filmed commercials must be retired after eighteen months; nevertheless, it is possible to make more than $4000 from one commercial, even working at scale. A few years ago a nine-year-old girl with no experience walked into an agent's office, was sent on an interview right away, and was hired on the spot to do a toothpaste advertisement. In a single day of toothy grins, nine different commercials were made, and a few years later she was richer by $27,000 for the day's experience.

Still, the working actor must generally be considered in terms of poverty, not riches. Thousands of people try to make a go of it in acting. A few get enough work to keep them going for years — a job here, a job there, a supplement here and there. Of these, only a very few make enough money, in ten years, to go to Sardi's or Ciro's for dinner instead of Howard Johnson's or the Taco Bell. We know that this probably does not interest you now, but will you still enjoy your tacos when you are forty-five?

FOUR

OTHER OPPORTUNITIES

If you've come this far, where are you? You feel ready to continue a career, and you have a home base, a photo-résumé, an agent, an interview technique, a few good prepared audition scenes, a union card, and a first job. You are at the beginning of a career. Here we leave you. You are now in touch with the sources that can give you the exact personal information and guidance you now need. Even at this point, you must remember that there is a 95 percent chance that you will fail at making a livelihood out of acting professionally. Face that fact realistically. In this chapter, we will examine the possibilities of acting professionally outside the established industries of entertainment. You might take a look.

Outside the industry

Everything in this book, so far, is about how an actor accommodates himself to the existing entertainment industries. The theatre, film and television industries have their own rules and procedures. "You've got to really be *sick* to want to be an actor here" says a well-known Hollywood agent. To be an actor means to stand, sit, smile, and squat on command, and often the command is given by a flagrantly dishonest and unethical old mogul.

It means spending most of your life looking for work — even when you are fifty — and most of your concentration on where the next job is coming from. It means *schlepping* on your time and at your expense from office to office, from casting director to casting director, and being emotionally and financially subject to a ruling elite in which you may have no personal interest or sympathy.

When you must audition and interview regularly for work (and when that work is both rarely won and transitory), you may begin to develop psychological problems. After all, it is *you* that you are auditioning with, and when rejection is piled atop rejection, something is bound to happen to you. Insecurity nibbles at your psyche. Every job you lose you attribute to a personal flaw. You either may retreat into a shell and self-destruct, or, conversely, stuff yourself with bluster and then fall prey to that. Actors who believe their own bluster become the most pathetic sights in New York and Hollywood; they have become the product they are selling.

Actors are people, and many must fight the contrary desires that war within them: the desire for security versus the lust for fame, the desire for personal happiness versus the need for artistic and emotional freedom. Many actors — even successful ones — find themselves virtual slaves to their profession, and unable to make a personal decision without first consulting their agents, their producers, and their managers. Others enslave themselves to a set of industry conventions that are brutally dehumanizing. The vast majority are poor almost to the point of starvation, and uncounted numbers of them go to jail every year for theft, forgery, and narcotics transactions. In such an unstable atmosphere, homosexuality, pandering, and prostitution flourish. Is this really the world you want to enter? You can see why your parents paled when you told them you wanted to be an actor.

More and more people, however, are finding acting careers outside of the acting industries today. For those lusting for stardom, these alternatives will not be acceptable, and for countless others they are a compromise.

Educational theatre

The first alternative is what is generally called educational theatre. While America does not have a national theatre, we do have a series of publicly supported theatres in the nation's colleges and universities. These, which began as academic branches of English and speech departments in the 1930's, 40's, and 50's, have become in our time producing organizations which, within obvious limitations, advance live theatre and film art in surprising ways. Numerous professional theatre artists now associate themselves with university theatre establishments, partly for the financial security and prestige that such positions can bring, and partly to have the freedom to work without commercial limitations.

A position with a university drama department will generally require you to teach acting, directing, playwriting, dramatic literature, or theatre technique on a regular basis for the nine-month academic year. You may also be asked to direct plays with students and even to act in them. Depending on the institution, you ordinarily have a high degree of freedom to teach and direct what material you choose. In return for this you are given a reasonable annual salary and, at most institutions, a position with eventual job security (tenure). Drama professors at the top of their profession may earn sizable salaries (over $25,000 at the best institutions) and may be eligible for chairmanships and deanships if they desire to move into administrative areas. There is also the excitement of working with young people and the three months off every year, together with occasional sabbatical leaves with full pay that generally provide another three months off every three years.

Since university theatres are admittedly not wholly professionalized, the position entails more academic credentials than does a Broadway or Hollywood career. Many schools expect their drama faculties to publish books and articles about their specialty — the "publish or perish" formula which has angered so many in the arts and letters faculties of American colleges. More enlightened universities, however, permit their drama staffs to contribute in ways other than publication: by directing plays and acting in them, for example, or by writing plays and filmscripts. This regulation at bottom is a good one; it encourages theatre faculties to strive for a professional level in their various disciplines. The best teachers of acting and directing, one would expect, are those who can move easily between professional and academic engagements, even if they choose not to do so.

Very few people can combine a career in educational theatre with another in the professional world, unless the university which employs them also operates a professional program. Many try for the best of both worlds: the security of teaching and the glamor and riches of Hollywood or Broadway stardom, but very few succeed. In order to do either well, you must have a massive commitment to it. You can hardly work full-time as a university drama professor and audition for Hollywood or Broadway roles between classes. A combination of the two careers, however desirable in theory, is extremely difficult to pull off in practice. One or the other must dominate.

If you are interested in pursuing a career in educational theatre you must go to graduate school, and beyond that you should do everything in your power to get a doctoral degree: either a DFA or a PhD. Either of these degrees involves a great deal of reading and writing (as well as some acting and directing), and usually the acquisition of one or two foreign languages as well. Do not even think about it if you are not already a dedicated student. Today the MFA degree, which involves less academic work than the doctorate, is also accepted as a valid teaching degree at many smaller colleges and some big ones. As a result, many students prefer to go job hunting at colleges with an MFA in hand, though their prospects frankly are more limited. It is true that many colleges accept non-degreed members for faculty drama positions, but these require enormous proven talent and ability, usually demonstrated by standing as a nationally known artist.

Successful university drama instructors are invariably people who have a love for teaching, for academic freedom, and for the university life. Teaching, on the other hand, may be a very unhappy alternative for the person captivated by the wish to act professionally. A university instructor is not a professional actor or director but a professional educator, and would-be actors that go to graduate school in order to get a degree "to fall back on" if they fail to make it may never find much satisfaction on a college campus. No matter how professionalized, the academic program is still one of scrutiny and analysis as much as it is of production and performance. It is fascinating to anyone driven by curiosity and a desire for knowledge; it is a supreme bore to anyone looking only for the thrill of the followspot and the fan magazine. It probably involves as much effort to become a successful professor as a successful actor, so it is not recommended that any budding actor "fall back" on the profession of teaching.

Detriments of a college teaching career may be snobbery, affectation, and political intrigue, as in any other field. Drama departments tend to be neurotically split between academic and professional interests, and the Shavian dictum, "If you can, do; if you can't, teach," strikes a note of terror in the hearts of many academicians. Still, the climate is brisk, the battles electric, and the sense of artistic fulfillment in directing and teaching is considerable for the right person.

Doing your own thing on stage

For the performer who wants to create and perform, but has little or no interest in academia, there is a third alternative between the profession and the campus, and that is the private, non-union theatre company. Some of the most exciting and artistic work in America is currently being done by these companies, current examples of which are the Performance Group in New York, the Living Theatre in and around Europe, The San Francisco Mime Troupe, the Company Theatre in Los Angeles, the South Coast Repertory Theatre in Costa Mesa, California, and various experimental groups gathered around a key figure or leader like Joseph Chaikin, Paul Sills, or Andre Gregory.

These theatres operate outside the established unions or industry. Naturally such groups may have a short life, but some develop an enviable measure of security. Many are communal in both art and living arrangements. Most of these groups perform without salaries and simply try to make ends meet at the box office. Occasionally they are helped out by small grants, and from time to time they establish themselves in a big way and make some money, as Paul Sills's *Story Theatre* group did.

Nothing prevents you from looking up and joining one of these groups, if they will take you, and nothing prevents you from starting up your own. All it takes is a building, some friends, some paint and plywood and some energy and ideas. True, you will have to work in the daytime at "regular" jobs in order to be free to rehearse at night, but if you are doing what makes you happy, you will be well rewarded. For most people the urge to perform need not be satisfied by working on Broadway, in Hollywood, or on the Yale Drama School stage; it could be quite satisfactorily fulfilled by acting with friends before a small audience in your own home town. You should certainly consider this before you pack your bags for either coast. Some of the most genuinely artistic work in the country is done at theatres like these.

As it is true with the theatre, so is it true with the film. The rapid growth of independent, non-studio filmmaking has been one of the outstanding features of the 60's and early 70's in America; and a large group of non-union amateur filmmakers is growing up nationwide. They have a literature, a character, and an opportunity to exchange presentations. Student and amateur films are being commercially marketed, too, so that a venture into independent filmmaking does not necessarily cut off all professional possibilities.

Even television is opening up into an area of amateur exploitation. Local community antenna television systems (CATV) are initiating local, closed-circuit non-union programming. Coupled with the expected revolution occasioned by cassette broadcasting and the home television systems now appearing on the market, television is no longer going to be under the strict rule of the network executives and sponsors that dominate the industry. Via the nationwide Public Broadcasting System (an association of educational television stations), some of these amateur works may eventually gain a larger audience.

The upshot of the contemporary decentralization in theatre, film, and television is to weaken somewhat the position of the entertainment industries. Though they still remain fiercely dominant, side routes to performing careers have opened up. The big studios are selling off their back lots and their wardrobes. Broadway and off-Broadway are down in attendance and number of productions, and off-off-Broadway is up. Television networks are now restrained by the Federal Communications Commission so that they may offer only three hours of prime time network programming nightly instead of three and a half (effective 1972). Everywhere we see a grass roots movement towards artistic expression, unhindered by the industry and reaching for greater exposure.

Undoubtedly the industry will prevail, if only by incorporating, little by little, the changes outside of it. America is a land of corporate amalgamation, and there is no reason to believe that home television will escape the jurisdiction of the unions that will vie for its control — a struggle that is already proceeding. But the artistically dedicated performer must consider this question: Does the industry really serve my purpose, or would I be happier doing my own thing somewhere else?

Acting in the real world

There is a final alternative. For many actors — including all those who are not appearing in or preparing for a production — it is a forced alternative. And that is acting on the largest stage, the stage of life itself.

Acting in the real world is a controversial subject. Unlike work in the entertainment industries, it is not a well-documented or well-defined activity, and to many people it is suspect. What is the difference between acting in life and being a charlatan, a confidence man who preys on the good will of others? Before offering some answers to this question, we may reflect on the attractiveness of acting.

Nobody goes into acting just for the money. There are very few other professions about which one can make that statement. When Jean-Louis Barrault, the French producer, was chided by an auto manufacturer about his long hours and mediocre wages, Barrault replied, "Yes, but if you weren't paid for it, would you continue to build automobiles?" "Of course not!" said the manufacturer. "You see," said Barrault, "I would still act, and there is the difference between us."

For at least some part of the time, we all desire to live life to the hilt: to be totally aware of ourselves and our surroundings and to leave a mark on the world around us. We passionately want this, yet life seems so niggling in its opportunities. Life is chaotic, with unformed characterizations, confused expositions, poorly built climaxes, and sloppy dénouements.

Well, there is the stage! It is life clarified and intensified. Here are love as it should be felt, death as it should be suffered, speeches that men should speak. Whatever our motivations for wishing to live a life that has vibrancy and good dramatic order, the stage satisfies them. Like Barrault, we will sacrifice money and comfort to gain what the stage can offer. And that is why so many actors feel that they will simply die if they cannot act. And that is also why acting to many of its practitioners is virtually a sacred art, with its own saints: Stanislavski, Chaplin, Duse, Olivier, and Garbo.

But what if an actor cannot satisfy his needs for intense, dramatic experience? What if there are no productions and no set roles — paid or unpaid — available to him? Why should he not enjoy the pleasures of performance in real life? "All the world's a stage," says our playwright, "and all the men and women merely players. They have their exits and their entrances, and one man in his time plays many parts."

Surely, a thoughtless or exploitative performance can turn life into melodrama or even tragedy. The actor in everyday events needs a sense of fair play. But so does everyone else, for life causes all people to perform certain roles. Teachers act. Salesmen act. Daughters act in relation to their mothers, and husbands in relation to their wives. In *The Presentation of Self in Everyday Life*, the prominent sociologist Erving Goffman describes many ways in which people provide their own stage settings (homes, offices, etc.), costumes (clothing, shoes, etc.), and modes of performance. The question is not whether a person should take on various roles in everyday life, but whether he should do so with skill and relish rather than walking through his part.

There is a further reason for consciously acting in the real world. Besides the inevitability of roles, there is the inevitable human need to communicate with others. In all communications, including those in which roles are unimportant, a person faces the task of translating inner impulses into outward behavior. He may wish to appear honest, learned, artistic, sensitive, kind, compassionate, sexy, mean, hungry, detached, religious, threatening, etc. Somehow, he must try to express his wish in behavior, to be his own playwright and director and actor so that he may get his wish across to his audience, even an audience of one. He may do so with little skill or awareness, but, if he is experienced as a stage actor he may bring great talent to his communications and may be well rewarded for his performance by the response of his audience.

Communications as simple as asking for the time of day carry implications about the speaker's inner life and his expectations for others. The psychologist Eric Berne has defined some subtle and harmful patterns of communication in *Games People Play*. Again, the question is not whether a person should "perform" in interpersonal relations — that is inevitable — but whether he should do so with verve and understanding.

An actor who chooses to exercise his art in the real world does face a difficulty. Although he cannot be accused of insincerity toward others — *all* people act both in social roles and in translating their inner impulses into personal communications — he can be accused of fooling himself. What if he becomes the part he chooses to play?

The risk is real. It happens to professional actors. But for a person who has decided to use his acting abilities on the stage of life, the risk seems slight. He more than others recognizes that out of the chaos of existence we write our own scenarios, with no playwright to fall back on. He knows that we design our scenery, cast our characters, and enact our complications, crises, and resolutions. He recognizes that there is rarely an artistically satisfying dénouement or a standing ovation at the end. And he is aware of the rewards for himself and those around him when life is vivid and memorable. In contrast, the rewards of acting professionally may seem slight indeed.

APPENDIX

This is a skeletal book. It is not our intention to provide, in an appendix or elsewhere, a series of addresses which will quickly go out of date, or information that might prove factually incorrect. Besides, it will be your job, and you may as well start now, to locate the people you will need to provide you with current factual information on your career. We will, however, help you get started. The following addresses are your first contact points with the industries.

Published information

In New York you can find virtually any material published about acting, including trade papers, journals, and books, at the Drama Book Shop, 150 West 52nd Street (just off Seventh Avenue). You should certainly head there immediately upon arrival in New York. The employees of the Book Shop are usually actors themselves and can offer you good advice. Trade papers are also sold regularly at news stands in the Times Square area.

In Los Angeles you may pick up trade papers around any of the motion picture studios, or at the big outdoor magazine stand at the corner of Las Palmas and Hollywood Boulevard. Many bookstores line Hollywood Boulevard. One that specializes in your interests is Larry Edmunds' Cinema and Theatre Book Shop, at 6658 Hollywood Boulevard.

Books listing agencies, producers, theatre owners, etc., come out every so often and are available at these outlets. These are *Simon's Directory of Theatrical Materials, Services and Information*, the *Madison Avenue Handbook*, and *Madison Avenue West*. These books contain much information you do not need, but some that you may find valuable, particularly listings of producers of television commercials. Look these books over before you buy, for they are in the $5.00 range.

Lists of franchised agents and producers

Lists of agents are available at the following union offices, but you must pick them up in person.

In New York:

Actors' Equity Association, 165 West 46th Street, 10036.

Screen Actors' Guild, 551 West 52nd Street, 10019.

American Federation of Television and Radio Artists, 724 Fifth Avenue, 10019.

In Los Angeles:

Actors' Equity Association, 6430 West Sunset, 90028.

Screen Actors' Guild, 7750 West Sunset, 90046.

American Federation of Television and Radio Artists, 1551 North LaBrea, 90028.

For a start, you can simply find agency listings in the classified sections of the Manhattan and Los Angeles telephone directories, available in your hometown library or telephone company office. Look under "Theatrical Agencies."

Lists of producers are not available from the unions, but you can find most of them in *Simon's Guide* or a similar publication. A less complete (but still valuable) list is also in the yellow pages of the telephone directories of Manhattan and Los Angeles under the heading "Theatrical Managers and Producers." ("Theatrical" in this case applies to all producers — those of television programs, films, and commercials as well as live theatre.) In New York, you can buy the geographical guides to agents and producers, which list them by street as well as alphabetically. These guides, which are published and updated regularly, are available at the Drama Book Shop, and are a must. They are *Agents by Building* ($1.35) and *The Geographical Casting Guide* ($1.75).

Lists of summer theatres

There are about 350 summer theatres in annual operation in this country, and they offer programs which differ enormously. Some are all-Equity companies with stars, and with budgets in the six-figure range. Others are rustic playhouses where the actors live in a barn and build sets between rehearsals (for no pay). A fairly complete list of summer theatres, with pertinent information about their programs, apprenticeships, and the like may be found in *The Summer Theatre Directory,* published annually by the American Theatre Association, Inc. It is available in spring from their offices at the John F. Kennedy Center, Suite 5225, 726 Jackson Place, N.W., Washington, D.C. 20566, or from the Drama Book Shop in New York. A similar work, called *Summer Theatre,* is available where trade papers are sold in New York, or from the publisher *(Show Business)* at 136 West 44th Street, New York 10036.

Lists of regional repertory theatres

There are more than thirty regional theatres presently in year-round operation (at least eight months of the year). They are loosely federated in a League of Resident Theatres and hire their actors under a special Equity contract. These theatres tend to have a fairly short life, since they depend on the irregularities of local support and national governmental and foundation assistance. The complete list of regional theatres in operation, together with their schedules, is available for 25¢ from the Theatre Communications Group, 20 West 43rd Street, New York 10036. Some of the oldest of these theatres are listed below.

Actor's Theatre of Louisville
North Seventh Street
Louisville, Kentucky 40202

Alley Theatre
615 Texas Avenue
Houston, Texas 77002

Alliance Theatre Company
1280 Peachtree Street N.E.
Atlanta, Georgia 30309

American Conservatory Theatre
450 Geary Street
San Francisco, California 94102

American Place Theatre
423 West 46th Street
New York, N.Y. 10036

American Shakespeare
Festival Theatre
1850 Elm Street
Stratford, Connecticut 06497

Arena Stage
Sixth and M Streets S.W.
Washington, D.C. 20024

Asolo State Theatre Company
(affiliated with URTA)
Postal Drawer E
Sarasota, Florida 33578

Barter Theatre
P. O. Box 250
Abingdon, Virginia 24210

Center Stage
11 East North Avenue
Baltimore, Maryland 21202

Center Theatre Group
(Mark Taper Forum)
135 North Grand Avenue
Los Angeles, California 90012

Cleveland Playhouse
2040 East Eighty-sixth Street
Cleveland, Ohio 44106

Goodman Theatre
The Art Institute of Chicago
200 South Columbus Drive
Chicago, Illinois 60603

Hartford Stage Company
65 Kinsley Street
Hartford, Connecticut 06103

Long Wharf Theatre
222 Sargent Drive
New Haven, Connecticut 06511

McCarter Theatre
University Place
Box 526
Princeton, New Jersey 08540

Manitoba Theatre Center
174 Market Avenue
Winnipeg, Canada

Meadow Brook Theatre
(also plays in Detroit)
Oakland University
Rochester, Michigan 48063

Milwaukee Repertory Theatre
Company
Performing Arts Center
929 North Water Street
Milwaukee, Wisconsin 53202

Minnesota Theatre Company
725 Vineland Place
Minneapolis, Minnesota 55403

Mummers Theatre
400 West Sheridan
Oklahoma City, Oklahoma 73102

Negro Ensemble Company
St. Mark's Playhouse
133 Second Avenue
New York, New York 10003

New York Shakespeare Festival
Public Theatre
425 Lafayette Street
New York, New York 10003

Playhouse in the Park
Mt. Adams Circle
Eden Park
Cincinnati, Ohio 45202

The Repertory Theater of
   Lincoln Center
Vivian Beaumont Theater
150 West 65th Street
New York, N.Y. 10023

Seattle Repertory Theatre
P.O. Box B
Queen Anne Station
Seattle, Washington 98109

Stage/West
1511 Memorial Avenue
West Springfield, Massachusetts
   01089

Stratford Shakespearean Festival
   (takes very few American actors)
Stratford, Ontario
Canada

Studio Arena Theatre
681 Main Street
Buffalo, New York 14203

Trinity Square Repertory Company
87 Weybosset Street, Room 320
Providence, Rhode Island 02903

Washington Theatre Club
1101 23rd Street N.W.
Washington, D.C. 20037

Schools of theatre and acting

Colleges and universities offering major programs in drama are numerous and located everywhere in the country. A complete list is available in the ATA Directory of American College Theatre, available at the American Theatre Association, Inc., John F. Kennedy Center, Suite 5225, 726 Jackson Place, N.W., Washington, D.C. 20566. Some colleges are principally graduate schools, while others are primarily undergraduate. Write to those you are interested in, and evaluate their programs and faculties comparatively.

At the risk of excluding some good ones, here is a list of several well-respected, permanent *commercial* schools that offer programs in acting.

In New York:

The American Academy of Dramatic Arts, 120 Madison Avenue, 10016. (Established 1884; offers a two year course in daytime or evenings to high school graduates.)

Herbert Berghof Studio, 120 Bank Street, 10014. (Established 1945; offers courses during four seasonal terms. You may sign up for as few or as many as you wish.)

Gene Frankel Theatre Workshop, 115 MacDougal Street, 10012. (Offers courses and workshop productions during four seasonal terms; admission by interview.)

Sonia Moore Studio of the Theatre, 251 West 80th Street. (Mailing
address: 485 Park Avenue, 10022. Offers a program during fall,
winter, and spring terms. Admission by interview.)
Neighborhood Playhouse, 340 East 54th Street, 10022. (Offers a full-
time program to high school graduates, during which students
"are not permitted to seek or accept engagements to appear
in public, either on the amateur or professional stage.")

In Los Angeles:

Columbia College, 925 North La Brea Avenue, Los Angeles 90038.
(Offers programs in television, film, and stage production.)
Laurence Merrick Studios, 870 North Vine Street, Hollywood 90038.
(Offers courses and programs in film acting and production.)
Theatre of Arts, 4128 Wilshire Boulevard, Los Angeles 90005.
(Offers courses day and night with terms beginning every two
months.)

All of these schools, of course, charge tuition (up to $1400 per year, down
to $20 per term, depending on school and courses) and have facilities
for study and work. Most present plays before invited audiences of producers and agents.

There are several drama conservatories in the United States, though
this is a relatively new development; these are college-level programs
that are not degree-oriented, and specialize in theatre instruction to the
exclusion of most or all other subjects. Several college campuses have
tried, with varying success, to incorporate conservatory-style programs
within their undergraduate curricula (New York University, the University of California at Irvine, and the University of Washington, for
example). Others begin as conservatories of drama and are not obligated
to teach toward a normal BA at all; they usually offer a BFA instead.
Among these are:

The Juilliard School, Department of Drama, Lincoln Center Plaza,
New York, 10023.
Goodman School of Drama, 200 South Columbus Drive,
Chicago, Illinois 60603.
California Institute of the Arts, 24700 McBean Parkway,
Valencia, California 91355.

Appendix

Where to live and eat
in New York and Los Angeles

There are many residences and restaurants in Los Angeles and New York
that cater to actors or to young people with little money. The YMCA and
YWCA offer rooms for men and women on a daily or weekly basis. The
main residential branches of these are:

In New York:

William Sloan House (YMCA), 356 West 63rd Street, 10023.

Studio Club (YWCA), 210 East 77th Street, 10021.

In Los Angeles:

Hollywood YMCA, 1553 North Hudson, 90028.

Studio Club (YWCA), 1215 Lodi Place, 90038.

The Y's offer sanitary accommodations, usually with a cafeteria on the
premises, for around $20 per week. Girls, in addition, can find New York
accommodations at The Rehearsal Club, 47 West 63rd Street, New York
10023, which caters exclusively to actresses.

But there are hundreds of cheap hotels and restaurants in both cities.
Fairly complete lists may be found in Arthur Frommer's widely available
books: *New York on $5.00 a Day* and *Hollywood and Los Angeles on
$5.00 and $10.00 a Day*. It is decidedly wise to make reservations (con-
firmed in writing) in advance of your arrival at any budget hotel.